CLASSIC
BOURBON, TENNESSEE
& RYE WHISKEY

CLASSIC
BOURBON, TENNESSEE
& RYE WHISKEY

JIM MURRAY

Dedicated to the one time Kings of Maryland, Aunt
Rose, Uncle Den, Denise and Barry, and all my dear
friends and neighbours in Kentucky

First published in 1998 in Great Britain by
Prion Books Limited
32-34 Gordon House Road,
London NW5 1LP

© PRION BOOKS LIMITED
Text copyright © Jim Murray 1998
Designed by DW Design

A CIP record for this book is available from the
British Library

ISBN 1-85375-218-5

Printed and bound in China

CONTENTS

INTRODUCTION

Opposite
Roadside
refreshment
Kentucky style
just outside
Frankfort.

And so there I was, talking to some 250,000 Scotsmen on their national radio station about all my journeys around the globe in search of whisk(e)y. Then the inevitable question was asked "OK Jim, so you've been to 150 distilleries, which country makes the best whisky in the world?" The interviewer was a Scotsman, the interviewee had about as Scottish a name as you are ever likely to find. To say the question was loaded is to put it mildly. "Well, er, if you must know..." I hesitated and then blurted out the truth. "Actually, it's Kentucky. The best whisky in the world is made there." I was nearly unplugged on the spot as a nation spluttered into its morning porridge.

I genuinely believe that if you take the new whiskey from each Kentucky distillery and inspect it before it is put into the bottle and then again when it is about six to eight years old, the average quality of that whiskey will be better than what you are likely to find in Scotland's malt distilleries (having inspected theirs at 10-12 years). This is not as surprising as it sounds: so few American distilleries are now operating there is very little room in the bourbon industry for error. I happily admit Scotland boasts the finest single whisky on earth with the incomparable

Ardbeg. And no bourbon, not even Ancient Age or Wild Turkey, can quite match the complexity of Scotland's very finest blends. But take your average bourbon and spend a bit of time learning its charms and secrets and you are in for a bigger treat than by doing likewise with an average malt. Certainly the sheer lip-smacking, tongue-rolling, tastebud-seducing deliciousness of the finest bourbon is a match for even the top Scotch blends.

Every bourbon (except Georgian) has three types of grain making an impression and the oak has a big say too. Rye, though, has to be my favourite whiskey style in the world. Not a week goes by without me tasting some magnificent peaty Islay malt and wondering if I prefer that. Then I taste some full-bodied, prisoner-dispatching rye and realise what I have in my hand is something almost too beautiful and awesome to describe adequately. Part of this book's purpose is to alert whisk(e)y lovers to what they are missing: in Britain, Europe and Africa rye is not available at all.

Having said all that, really it is futile to compare one type of whisky against another. You should compare like with like, which is what this book is all about. I've written many books on whisky, yet this was really the first I ever wanted to write: for so long have I been in love with this noble, indigenous American spirit. There have been one or two other books on bourbon over the years with tasting notes. But I'm proud to say that it is the first ever written principally as a tasting guide to bourbon, Tennessee and rye whiskey. Also it is the first ever written for international consumption. The history of the brands is important. But I felt that the book should be designed for the consumer as well as the connoisseur in mind. So these are the most in-depth bourbon tasting notes ever published.

You may not agree with all my assessments; I honestly hope you don't. The interest in bourbon is starting to boom and I hope this book will spark off some passionate discussion among whisk(e)y lovers. American whiskeys have been misunderstood and in some cases wholly ignored over the years, all to the connoisseur's loss.

It is not just the whiskey I love. It is also the culture that goes with it. And after all, where else do you get a country where the whiskey has been named after the man who did not own the distillery, but was just responsible for making its whiskey and is still living? There is even a tiny hamlet in the forested north of California as you head out towards Oregon called Whiskeytown, where whiskey was made and consumed a century-and-a-half ago.

As I hope this book will help you discover, the history of America and the spirit the country so proudly makes are indistinguishable. By drinking bourbon, Tennessee or rye you are experiencing a true taste of America.

THE SPIRIT OF THE FRONTIER

Opposite
The wild
abundance of
Kentucky's
bluegrass hills
tempted many a
pioneer to pull
up his wagon
and settle down.

"No populous city, with all the varieties of commerce and stately structures, could afford so much pleasure in my mind, as the beauties of nature I found here...Soon after, I returned home to my family with a determination to bring them as soon as possible to live in Kentucke, which I esteemed a second paradise..." So recalled pioneer and frontiersman Daniel Boone in 1784, reflecting on the magnetic charms of America's most glorious state. Even before bourbon was made there...

Yet by the time Boone was dictating his autobiography to friend John Filson, whiskey would have been a staple amongst his fellow

Kentuckians. It would not possibly have then been bourbon, as such, either by name or nature. That, as a distinctive whiskey type, was to arrive shortly after: Bourbon County from which the whiskey was eventually to take its name did not come into existence until 1785. But the distillation of a spirit from grain, which essentially whiskey is, would have been well practised and what they were drinking would have been a very close relation, a tasty template.

Right
Daniel Boone
(1735—1820)
and his fellow
pioneers brought
with them to
Kentucky the art
of whiskey
making.

The very first settlers determined to start life afresh in the wilderness of the west faced a hostile reception with native American Indians intent on repelling the pale faces. Losses on both sides were great and often achieved in the most appalling manner. Soon, though, the trickle of the bravest became a flood of the expectant and with numbers came safety. Many of these early settlers hailed from Virginia (of which Kentucky remained a part until at last gaining its independence in 1792, having begun the battle in the year of Boone's memoirs). Others travelled west from Pennsylvania. Boone, originally a Pennsylvanian, brought families through from North Carolina. Though quite different in character, the one thing Virginians and Pennsylvanians had in common was an ability to make whiskey. The North Carolinians, at that time, were no slouches, either.

When John Filson included Boone's story in his *Discovery of Kentucke* he also gave his own account of these promised lands as they stood in the early to mid 1780s. Although making no mention of the whiskey Boone's own relatives were already or soon to be making copious quantities of, he, significantly, tells of wild-rye growing in abundance while barley and oats had yet to be cultivated. He also mentions an "excellent beer" being made from the peas of the honey-locust tree.

Filson may not have mentioned it, but the plain truth is that the story of American whiskey is inextricably linked with the history of Kentucky and the romance of how the west was won. Since the 1750s tales had filtered back across the Appalachians of this wonderful land with rich soil and as much game as anybody could ever imagine or ever surely need. Boone was just one of a number of woodsmen and land developers determined to see just how true these stories were. He was not disappointed. A great many of those seeking a new life were those hardy Presbyterians, the Scotch-Irish. Often fleeing social and religious persecution, by 1776 a quarter of a million of them had crossed the Atlantic from Northern Ireland, Ulster, bringing with them to America the art and knowledge of distilling from grain, which they carried out to impressive effect in the western backwoods of Pennsylvania, Maryland and Virginia. Their first port of call had been New England but they had been made very unwelcome by the Puritanical element there and they ventured further inland in search of a home. It was not the Scotch-Irish ability to distil that the Puritans had little time for: in fact, it was probably the one thing they admired. From their very first landing in America the beer-imbibing Pilgrim Fathers set about trying to produce alcohol. They had no option. Water was regarded as the purveyor of disease and death, not the slaker of thirst, and when supplies ran low from their motherland they began brewing and distilling out of necessity.

Not all the Irish to enter America were Presbyterian. Many Catholics came too, and they knew every bit as much about making a fine whiskey. Of the multicultural migrants seeking a fresh life in America, only the Welsh did not possess a deep knowledge of distilling from grain, though, evidently, they soon learned.

When the first Kentucky outposts were erected, distilling apparatus was not far behind. Small stills could be carried by horse if the route they took followed Boone's trail through the Cumberland Gap, or, if their journey was from the north-east, aboard the flat-bottomed boats navigating the Monongahela and the Ohio. It is too often overlooked that this was an age when making your own spiritous liquor was a natural thing to do. All around the world, in the late 18th century, the art of distillation from both fruit and grain – and sometimes vegetable – was being practised and perfected. Even on the tiny and remote Pitcairn Island, the south Pacific hideaway of Fletcher Christian and his fellow mutineers on the Bounty, distilling was taking place: one of the renegade sailors had once worked at a Scottish distillery, though he had to make do with roots rather than malt. The end product, according to contemporary reports, was something similar in taste to whiskey.

Back in Kentucky, whiskey was being put to all kinds of uses. As well as rejuvenating flagging spirits when all looked lost, it was also used – as had been the case in Scotland, Ireland and Pennsylvania – to put excess grain to good use before it rotted. It was used to barter with Indians who often gratefully accepted it in exchange for fur, food and sometimes land. It was used as a medicine; would-be politicians tried to buy votes by offering their whiskey in

exchange; officers and soldiers were guaranteed a ration for defending forts; the builders of camps, like Lexington, were paid in part with Kentucky's rich fruit of the still. In virtually every walk of frontier life whiskey became the most valued of currencies.

But its importance did not apply exclusively to Kentucky. In parts of Tennessee whiskey actually came to be regarded as legal tender. In

Left
Whether for buying votes or paying cowhands whiskey became a prime currency in every walk of frontier life.

Pennsylvania it was deemed in some ways more vital still, important enough to cause what some regard as the very first civil war in the fledgling American nation.

The Whiskey Rebellion of 1794 deserves more than just a footnote in American history, which so often is all it receives. It was indicative in many ways of the mind of the people who had settled America. From 1786 there had been a

17

festering resentment amongst distilling farmers in western Pennsylvania against a national government determined to find funds to properly structure the country's industries in order for it to become a powerful trading nation. This was shared by those who drank this backwater whiskey and who were likely to have to pay more to do so. The Secretary for the Treasury, Alexander Hamilton, a staunch Federalist, hit upon the universally employed scheme of taxing the makers of distilled spirits, irrespective of whether their stills were used for commercial or personal use. For many braving it out in the farthest reaches of Pennsylvania, already dismayed by the lack of protection they were getting against continuing Indian raids, this was an insult they refused to tolerate. The last thing they needed was to be governed by a distant central government who seemed oblivious to the true worth, in bartering terms, of the whiskey they made. For some it was their lifeblood and amongst them were a number who had left Great Britain to escape the punitive taxes on whiskey there.

The first man unlucky enough to discover just how riled these farmers were was William Graham. In April 1786 he made the mistake of surfacing in Washington County, PA, and calling on distillers to tax them according to new laws. An angry mob grabbed him and dispossessed him of his pistols. He was then tarred, feathered and had his head shaven on one side. His humiliation was completed by his being forced to drink the now illegal whiskey the distillers made. The Excise Officer was then sent packing to report to his superiors, glad only that he was still alive to tell the tale.

It was a further six years before the full resentment of the distillers forced the President, General Washington (himself a rye distiller of repute), into full military action. It began when they attacked the home of the region's senior excise man, one of the distillers dying in the process. A dozen soldiers kept 500 or so farmers at bay at first. But then one was killed, and others were injured, surrendered or simply fled, and it was not long before the buildings were burned to the ground. Their emotions fully stirred, the western Pennsylvanians gathered 7,000-strong to march on Pittsburgh. And the insurrection was not confined to that state: pockets of distillers in Ohio, Maryland and, inevitably, Kentucky also caused unrest and marked their allegiance by erecting "liberty poles". Urged on by Hamilton, Washington finally put down the Whiskey Rebellion by bringing in 12,000 militia men, more, it is claimed, than were used to defeat the British. There were only a handful of deaths during the entire six years, although Hamilton was to meet a violent end in 1804 – he was shot dead in a duel with a political rival, none other than the country's Vice President Aaron Burr.

Right
George
Washington,
himself a distiller
of rye, was
finally forced to
quash the
six-year Whiskey
Rebellion using
12,000 militia
men.

Some distillers fled Pennsylvania for Kentucky where, by the early 1790s, they found a mature cottage, or cabin to be more precise, industry. One of the most influential early settlers of what is now central Kentucky, Colonel James Harrod, whose delightful town Harrodsburg stands today around where his small fort was erected, had already achieved the production of 35 bushels of wheat and 50 bushels of rye per acre some ten years before. Could he have been the very first Kentucky whiskey producer? Well, it's possible though highly unlikely as others are thought to have a greater claim. Where Harrod was known to have the ammunition, so to speak, other settlers had brought their artillery with them, 25-40-gallon pot stills. Some were even larger. At Harrodsburg is a mock fort showing how that community lived 200 years ago. In the graveyard next to it lie rows of broken, unmarked gravestones of Kentucky's very first settlers. Walk amongst them and you might, possibly, be strolling past the remains of Kentucky's very first, now unknown, whiskey maker.

The period between 1775 and the turn of the 19th century in many ways proved vital in the formation of bourbon whiskey. The families of some of today's most famous distilling names arrived on the scene in that short era, including the Boehms of Jim Beam fame, the Samuels of Maker's Mark, the Browns of Brown-Forman, plus the Peppers, Wellers, Haydens and Dants.

Another name you will see on bourbon bottles is that of Elijah Craig, who is often said to be Kentucky's first bourbon maker, though this was highly unlikely and there is no proof to support the claim. Certainly, one of the first to become widely known as a distiller was Isaac Shelby, Kentucky's first governor, but he was already

"Castle Lawn," Home of Mr. and Mrs. Fred B. Wacks, Fayette County, Kentucky

KENTUCKY'S KEY TO HOSPITALITY

Poet friend of ours describes OLD FITZ as "a bit of Ol' Kaintuck . . . distilled fragrance in bloom . . . the majestic sweep of bluegrass landscape . . . the pourable expression of Kentucky friendliness, good breeding, and hospitality." All this *in a bottle*, he says!

Could be . . . but we describe OLD FITZ in simpler terms. It is the best bourbon

we know how to make. In our century-old, family-owned distillery, each bottle receives our personal care. No expense is spared to give you a full-bodied, nut-flavored beverage which measures up to your idea of a truly satisfying drink.

All this you will find in OLD FITZGERALD genuine old fashioned bourbon. We invite you to try it.

BONDED
100 PROOF
KENTUCKY
STRAIGHT
BOURBON
WHISKEY

OLD FASHIONED... *but still in style*

OLD FITZGERALD
Stitzel-Weller Distillery, Inc. Louisville, Ky.

following in the footsteps of many before him. One Johnnie Boyd is considered to have been the first to have set up a still in the Cumberland region which spread between southern Kentucky and central Tennessee. So common were they to become in that area, that figures returned for Davidson County alone estimated that amongst the 4,000 people living there, 61 stills were in use.

It seems that every social historian looking into America's earliest times has tried and failed to discover the identity of the first person to make whiskey or bourbon. This, however, is fitting, because bourbon should not be identified with an individual; it should be thought of as a marker of its age and situation. It has been said before, and rightly so, that this divine American whiskey was not so much an invention as the product of an evolutionary process. And, perhaps it might be added, a symbiosis: Kentucky would not be Kentucky without bourbon; bourbon would not be bourbon without Kentucky.

Opposite
An Old Fitzgerald ad from the 1940s shows its whiskey as being as much a part of traditional Kentucky hospitality as the old colonial mansion.

THE SHAPING OF AMERICAN WHISKEY

Opposite
Ike Bernheim,
pictured in
1867, became
one of the biggest
names in
distilling, having
learned about
whiskey as a
peddler in
Pennsylvania.

During those evolutionary years for bourbon, the nation had to make do with other spirits which they held warmly in their hearts. Indeed, America's first commercial distilleries made rum, not whiskey. With the West Indies relatively close by, this was hardly surprising. Ships trading with the Caribbean brought first the spirit itself and then the sugar by-products required in its making as the continent's infant distilling industry got up and running. One certainly needed to: spirits imported into America were becoming too expensive for the colonists to buy. As well as rum, brandy also became popular. This was made from different fruits that the colonists planted, but none was better loved than the apple trees which grew in abundance, taking to

the New England soil as though they were indigenous. From these came applejack, to this day a much-enjoyed spirit, and cider which was quaffed in enormous quantities by seemingly all.

But it was only a matter of time before whiskey was being made, especially with the acceleration of those of Celtic origin arriving on North American shores. Before their arrival, though, American whiskey of the 17th century was not very different from what was to be made when the very first Kentucky distillers got down to business a century later. What was to eventually make the whiskey in Kentucky so different from any that had been made in America in the previous 70 years or so was the use of Indian corn, or maize as it is better known today. Early colonists even reported that it made a rather attractive beer. Maybe that was them being fanciful after having drunk stale ale which had travelled with them from Britain. Whatever, the settlers learned over time to fashion it into a bread and realised that despite the fact that it was very difficult to malt, whiskey could still be made from it, especially by adding a smaller percentage of other grain, like barley or rye, that could be malted. This would ensure the fermentation that is required to make any spirit. And from distilling from corn Kentuckians discovered by necessity a much lighter style of whiskey.

As the frontiers moved further and further west, Kentuckians knew that the whiskeys being drunk in the east were considerably heavier in character, hardly surprising seeing how rye was the principal ingredient. It was always likely that rye should be used to make whiskey because not only did the first settlers include the Scotch-Irish, but Germans as well and they had enjoyed a long history of using that grain in their homeland.

Above

A turn-of-the-century Louisville whiskey jug – often referred to by your grandpappy as his rheumatism medicine.

With the arrival of the 19th century came a more commercial approach to the making of whiskey. In Scotland and Ireland it had been simple: make your whiskey, legally or illegally, and get it to the nearest market as soon as possible. This was not quite so easy in Kentucky. For a start, and quite apart from its poor communication links, it was hard to know exactly what market Kentucky had. One of the reasons why the state decided to sever itself from Virginia's grasp was that its natural instinct was to trade westward, the direction in which its rivers ran. The established cities on the eastern seaboard saw their future exporting east. Stuck somewhere between the two were the Pennsylvanians who, before the advent of bourbon, made undisputedly the best whiskey in the country, especially in an area in Washington County where the first sparks setting off the

Whiskey Rebellion flew. The area took its name from the river which ran through it, Monongahela, and the fine rye whiskey made there was, in turn, called by that name. Even by 1810, Kentucky had a lot of catching up to do: despite that state being by now the home of around 400,000 souls, half of Pennsylvania's, the north-eastern state produced six and half million gallons of spirit that year, three times that of Kentucky. The choicest was known as Old Monongahela, Monongahela Rye or simply Monongahela Whiskey, and was almost certainly the very first American whiskey to be actually recognized as an indigenous style (some Kentuckians made a self-styled "Irish" whiskey, also using rye) and was advertised in the earliest newspapers of its day, becoming especially popular in settlements along and surrounding the Mississippi valley. Part of its attraction was that whoever bought it knew exactly what they were getting. The further west you travelled, the types of whiskey available depended on the excess materials at the still owners' disposal. Until the 1820s the whiskey in Kentucky and parts of Tennessee was a hotchpotch, sometimes – though rarely – made entirely of rye, entirely of corn or a mixture of both, though at no set percentage. Another reason why Monongahela gained such popularity in the west was because a first rule of whiskey production was to find markets away from where "apple whiskey" and brandy were in the greatest demand; it was a case of selling to the already converted. The most popular of all, Monongahela whiskey, came from Brownsville and some from there was sent as far as New Orleans, over a thousand miles as the crow flies, a lot longer by river boat. And by 1812 American whiskey was being exported as far afield as the Philippines and China.

Clearly American distillers were getting organized. Distillers in Scotland and Ireland had little help from learned sources as they forged their own particular whiskey industries. One George Smith from Kendal wrote a book on distilling published in London in 1723 that was practically useless for anyone distilling from barley, though it was required reading for anyone trying to whip up a cure for the Black Death. In Philadelphia, however, Harrison Hall's *Distiller* (following up on Michael Kraft's *The American Distiller* of 1804) had hit upon the topic of its time. Here was a book given over predominantly to the practical side of distilling whiskey, written by a distiller of whiskey whose years of experience could be drawn upon by anyone wishing to make the making of whiskey more than just a pastime. Even on the fly pages at the back of my copy can be seen the neat, copperplate hand of a potential distiller, working out the economic viability of Hall's wisdom:

600 bushels of corn at 20 $1.20	$4.80
150 bushels of rye at 371/2 .57	Cr 2000 gal whisky (sic)
1/2	30????
50 malt and hops.20	$6 0000
50 barrels at 75.37 1/2	1 00:hogs
grinding.50	7 00
wages to distiller.75	4 80
wood.20	2 20 profit in 90 days.
Leakages &???????????? 1.00	

From these equations, it appears the distiller has taken heed of Hall's opinion: "I have ever considered the union of rye and corn in mashing, as productive of more spirit and of purer quality, than can be obtained from either grain alone; and if the proportion of one fourth part of rye can be obtained, it is enough." There is a significance to these jottings: what is unquestionably being potentially made here is the forerunner of bourbon whiskey. That name still did not exist and it would later include malted barley, which at this time was virtually impossible to find in Kentucky; a visitor to the state in 1802 reported that all the rye grown was used in the making of whiskey (he did not mention, though, that what little barley there was was used in brewing beer). But what is interesting is the use of hogs – hogshead barrels – which Hall himself makes a point of referring to in great detail. He mentions briefly their use in maturation (although maturation did not come into the scheme of things as the idea was to make the stuff and then sell it as quickly as possible). But in more detail he describes how hogsheads were used for mashing, where boiling water was added to the ground grain, and fermentation, the process where yeast is added to produce alcohol. After dismissing the merits of using certain woods for the making of a hog, he recommends the use of white oak, which, he reckoned, should be scorched on the inside to prevent possible contamination during fermentation.

Distillers also used these charred hogs for storing and transporting their spirit. So now we have corn, malted rye, yeast and charred white oak barrels. And, what is more, Hall and contemporary reports from newspapers, show that sour mash had been discovered by the early 19th century – the method in which "return" (the spent solids from the distilled whiskey) was added to the mash in order to keep down acidity and prevent it from spoiling in the heat and humidity. What we have here, though still unnamed, is unquestionably bourbon whiskey.

Curiously, the prices of grain quoted by the potential distiller in the back of my copy of Harrison Hall's *Distiller* were a lot lower than examples given by Hall, showing that even then fluctuations in the market would alter the price of making whiskey. Yet it is worth remembering that a basic law for making whiskey in America was as true for the pioneers of two centuries ago as it is for distillers today: a spirit distilled from corn is much cheaper than one made from rye.

The thirst of the Kentucky distiller to acquire a knowledge of how to distil well and economically was very strong. A second book emerged, this one by Anthony Boucherine called *The Art of Making Whiskey*. It first appeared in 1819, the year after Hall's work and again published in Philadelphia. This time, though, a second publisher, based in Lexington, Kentucky, also took the book on.

Right
Ship'em out – transporting hogs and bottles of Dickel's Cascade in 1932. Barrels were charred at first only to prevent the whiskey from becoming contaminated.

With practical knowledge to be gained from neighbouring farmers and distillers and now text books to help them on their way, commercial distillers in Kentucky never looked back. And on 26 June 1821 the *Western Citizen* newspaper in Paris, Bourbon County, published its historic ad' for "Bourbon Whiskey", using the term for the very first time. Stout and Adams of Maysville were offering to sell it by the barrel or keg.

The Bourbon County of the 1820s stretched as far as the Ohio river, where Maysville was situated, and this great river was to play an

important part in the future of the whiskey industry. The early settlement of Ohio Falls had by now sprawled into a city called Louisville and further north on the opposite bank grew Cincinnati. The Ohio was to be the arterial route for Kentucky distillers to move their wares across country and to bigger markets until the arrival of the railroads during the 1850s and 60s.

As we have seen, it was during the crucial first half century of whiskey distilling in Kentucky that the form of bourbon was slowly shaped. But

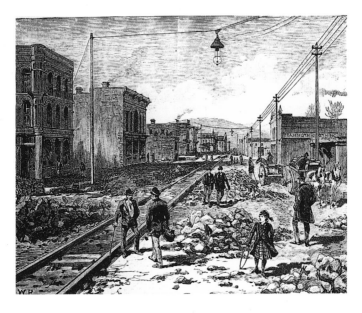

it would be over the following 60 to 70 years that bourbon would be indelibly defined as a whiskey style and for this there were two significant reasons. Whether by accident or design, it had been discovered that bourbon improved with ageing. It must have seemed odd to distillers in both the east and west when they heard favourable reports of their spirits from distant customers who wanted more. The distiller would often only taste the spirit fresh from the still but their customer might have received it several months old, its ageing accentuated by slopping around in the cask en route. In 1814 came Kentucky's first known advert for aged whiskey, a two-year-old, and five years later a seven-year-old was being touted. Neither, though, was described as bourbon. Without doubt, though, the benefits of ageing had been discovered.

The second breakthrough came with the introduction of continuous distillation. On both sides of the Atlantic it was known that while copper pots heated by fire were useful for making high-quality spirit, they were expensive and time-consuming to run. The race to invent a still which did not need cleaning out with every charge was on and the Americans were just about ahead of the Scottish and Irish. As early as 1790 the Philadelphian Colonel Alexander Anderson, showed off his new invention to none other than Thomas Jefferson. He had hit upon the idea of using steam to extract the alcohol from the beer, a principle perfected by distillers in Scotland, Ireland, Kentucky and Canada (where the massive Gooderham and Worts Distillery in Toronto employed wooden stills) over the following decades.

It was the bigger distillers who employed this new-fangled method; for a long time most Kentucky distillers were happy to make do the old-fashioned way, and it is not as easy as it might be to trace the development of these American distillers. When the individual histories of most of Kentucky's counties in the 1870s and 80s were written, the author kept one eye on his pen, the other on his social standing.

Left
Middlesborough Kentucky, 1890. Before the railroad came, taking Kentucky's whiskey to a wider audience, distillers had relied on the mighty Ohio river to get their wares to market.

With the Temperance movement becoming such a force, it was not always advisable to be seen to be advocating this sinful industry by writing about it. This affected many writers right up until the repeal of Prohibition.

However, the owners of Interstate Publishing had no such qualms when in 1883 they recounted the History of Daviess County, an area of Kentucky including Owensboro, a healthy distilling town on the banks of the Ohio. By giving a brief outline of the city's distilleries it was shown that by then companies had grown in size, one being able to accommodate 6,000 barrels of maturing stock, another being worth $87,000, a major employer, and contributing to the town's wealth.

Below
The first Stitzel Bros. distillery at 26th and Broadway, Louisville, Kentucky, 1872.

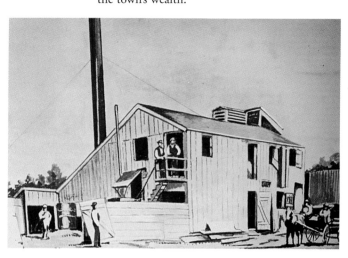

But what we should be most grateful for is the inclusion in the volume of the diary of Joseph Thomas – a depressing chronicle of misery and mishap. Amongst details of murders, lynchings, earthquakes and deaths by cholera, typhoid, small-pox and other assorted diseases that ravaged the people of Kentucky during its first century, are the following entries:

21 March 1873 – boiler exploded at M.V. Monarch's distillery and flew into the river, 200 or 300 yards distant.

10 April 1880 – the still-house, corn and cattle-shed of John Hanning distillery were consumed by fire; loss over $6,000.

5 September 1880 – N. M. Lancaster & Co's large new distillery was destroyed by fire; loss $25,000.

Because of the combustible nature of whiskey spirit and fumes arising from the still, fires at distilleries (themselves often little more than log cabins or shacks) were commonplace from the earliest times, and there were casualties along the road. But, there again, very little of note has ever been achieved without sacrifices along the way. And to those early distillers who so beautifully shaped the American whiskies we know today, we should be eternally grateful.

MAKING BOURBON

It is surprising just how often people outside of North America ask me if bourbon is actually a whiskey. Often it is regarded as some dark spirit as far removed from an easily identifiable dram like Scotch or Irish as rum and brandy. Bourbon, like rye, is a whiskey because it has been distilled from grain and has passed all the provisions placed on it by law in order to be so called.

The American Bureau of Alcohol, Tobacco and Firearms currently demands: 'Bourbon whisky' (sic), 'rye whisky', 'wheat whisky', 'malt whisky' or 'rye malt whisky' are whiskies produced at not exceeding 160 degrees proof from a fermented mash of not less than 51 per cent corn, rye, wheat, malted barley, or malted rye grain, respectively, and stored at not more than 125 degrees proof in charred new oak containers...whiskies...which have been stored in the type of oak containers prescribed, for a period of two years or more shall

be further designated as 'straight'; for example, 'straight bourbon whisky'. So, in the Blue Grass land of the thoroughbred, there you have it from the horse's mouth...

The way bourbon distillers go about achieving this result has now become fairly standard practice, yet each distiller does something a little different from the others, be it the percentage of grains used, the length of fermentation time, the temperature at which certain grains are mashed and so on.

Making malt whisky in Scotland is a rather

more straightforward affair: there they exclusively use malted barley and the pot distillation may vary between the common double distillation and the rarer triple distillation. In Ireland the flavouring technique is getting closer to the Kentucky style: distillers at the Midleton distillery, responsible for Jameson, Powers and Paddy brands, add unmalted barley to the mash. The more unmalted barley used, the stronger, sharper and fruitier the flavour. Again pot stills are used, but to a triple distillation method only.

In Kentucky the more rye added to the mashbill the more powerful, stark and sometimes rich the flavour is likely to be. The one big difference in bourbon distilleries is that they use continuous stills, and so make their whiskey in a much more efficient manner but with less contact with copper, the metal that is unquestionably the key that unlocks a spirit's flavours. The single exception to the rule is the recently re-opened Labrot and Graham distillery, which has installed three pot stills for triple distillation.

At all bourbon distilleries the grain is crushed individually and then added to boiling water in what is known as the three-step process. Because malted barley must be used in the mashing process, this is always treated tenderly and is entered last as the water cools. Where once most towns had their own maltings, it is today a very specialised process. Malted barley

Left
A beer still at the Stitzel Weller distillery.

is barley that has been steeped in cold water until it doubles in weight, and then slowly air dried and regularly turned during the process. In simple terms the barley has been tricked into growing and so the carbohydrates are turned into sugars. It is these sugary enzymes which will be fed upon by the yeast, producing equal measures of alcohol and carbon dioxide. And it is believed that one of the reasons why Kentucky's limestone-shelf water is so good in

the brewing process, is that the rich nutrients dissolved into the water also enrich the yeast.

The corn which makes up the majority of the mashbill has a very tough outer wall. For that reason it is cooked to a very high temperature, and often under pressure, to help break down those cellular walls. Rye – or wheat if preferred – is not malted in the making of bourbon. So some distillers might even add this in with the corn for high temperature boiling, but most wait until the water has cooled. This, they believe, releases

most flavour, though at Barton, where the rye is boiled to the highest temperatures, the whiskey has a distinctly peppery flavour.

The mashing stage is so called because, just as when you mash tea, the idea is for the water to leach all the flavours possible from the grain. With the malt the aim is to extract as much sugar as possible. It is also at this stage that the sour mash process is introduced (adding an amount of backset, that is the spent grains from the previous distillation, the thin stillage, to the mash). This succeeds in controlling the acidity of the mash and helps prevent bacterial infection. Visit any distillery and it is easy to discover just why this is called sour mash. When the mash is first poured into the fermenters it is sweet on account of the sugars leached from the malt. As the yeast works on the mash the more alcohol-rich it becomes and sour to taste.

Even this bubbling of the fermenting beer yields some surprising secrets. Jimmy Russell after 40 years at Wild Turkey, is actually able to tell just how long the mash has been fermenting to within a few minutes just by the shape the

Left
Hypnotic stuff –
distillery workers
tend the yeast
tub at the W L
Weller and Son,
1932.

bubbles take at any one time. It is a truly remarkable and awesome art. To do this you have to know your own distillery, for at each distillery, a different length of time is taken to ferment, in order to hit a particular distillation slot. The speed of fermentation can be controlled by pipes through which cool water runs, though the distilleries that do not have this apparatus precool their mash before it enters the fermenters. The colder the fermentation, the longer it takes to complete. Finally, when the last bubbles have died down it is ready for distillation. This yellow-brown goo is now known as beer and this enters the first still, the beer still, complete with solids. In the case of continuous stills this beer, which falls from the top of the still, is met by an upward blast of steam which strips away the alcohols. To slow the fall the still is fitted with a number of plates which also allow the steam to pass through. After this alcohol-rich vapour re-condenses it is passed through a doubler, a simple form of pot still, where the strength is marginally increased. The result is white dog, clear bourbon designate.

By law the strength at this stage cannot be any higher than 160 proof, 80 per cent alcohol by volume (abv), in order that it retains as much character as possible. The higher the strength the spirit is distilled to, the purer the alcohol. Then the spirit is reduced in strength to, again by law, a maximum 125 proof and stored in virgin oak casks. These casks have to be charred from the inside. This causes fissures and allows the spirit free access to some juicy fresh wood and extracts various chemicals. The greater the char, the darker the whiskey is likely to become in the shortest space of time.

Unlike in Scotch, Irish, Canadian, Japanese and virtually every other whiskey in the world, bourbon, and likewise rye, cannot have any artificial colouring added. When the spirit is filled into the cask it is as clear as water. It is what happens over the following four, six, eight or even twelve years that places bourbon amongst the three most distinctive whiskey styles in the world, along with rye and the peaty Islay malts of Scotland.

Kentucky is not only a beautiful land, it is one that is at the mercy of the elements at their most belligerent: from extremely hot summers where temperatures soar into the hundreds and the percentage humidity is not far behind, temperatures crash in the winters to around minus twenty and sometimes below. It is for that reason that, traditionally, bourbon was made in season, Spring and Fall. In summer the water supplies dried up, in winter they were frozen solid. The spring can also be tornado season which, thankfully rarely, has also been known to have an effect on whiskey – a terminal one, by tossing barrels of it into the air and smashing them into the ground.

Because of the very high summer temperatures barrels stored at the top of warehouses mature faster on account of being cooked faster. During this period I have been on the top floors of some warehouses and recorded temperatures in excess of 125°F. Likewise, barrels kept on the lower floors will mature slower. For this reason it is not uncommon to see some distillers move barrels from one part of the warehouse to another to even up the scores. However, this is a labour-intensive and therefore costly practice which is becoming rarer. There are two types of warehouse, firstly the brick, which manages to keep a little cooler when the going gets hot, and old ironclads which tend to offer the highest temperatures, especially in the buzzard roosts, the highest point of the building. These spots are useful for maturing whiskey very quickly.

The whiskey reaches perfection when a balance has been struck between the flavours extracted from the wood (this has a bigger say than Scotch and Irish, who use second-hand casks) and the grains used in the mashing. Knowing just where to choose the barrels and when, especially for the selection for single barrel bottlings, is a craft every bit as impressive and skilful as a blender's. And, funnily enough, those distillers who have worked quite a few years at their distillery, seem to have an uncanny knack of picking some stunningly impressive barrels.

Below
The old ironclad warehouses at Stitzel Weller.

Each distillery has their own set way of doing things. The following is a breakdown of how the distilleries make their bourbon:

KENTUCKY

Above
End of the line
– bottling
Old Judge in
turn-of-the-
century
Frankfort,
Kentucky.

ANCIENT AGE

Corn from Indiana and Kentucky; rye from north-western states; barley malt from Minnesota. Mashing water from Kentucky River, heated to 110°F then corn added and cooked under pressure to 240°F, cooled down to around 180°F when rye is added, cooled to 152°F for malt. Further cooled to about 64°F then pumped to fermenter where small amount of backset with yeast is added. Further backset is pumped in to

take the amount up to approx. 33 per cent. The twelve copper alloy steel fermenters each hold 92,000 gallons. Fermentation time: 4-5 days. Single beer still: seven foot copperless, stainless steel. Condenser: all copper. Doubler: stainless steel with a copper condenser.

BARTON

Corn from Elizabethtown, Indiana and Kentucky; rye from Minnesota; barley malt from South Dakota and Minnesota. Mashing water supplied partly from local spring, mostly from Teurs Lake. Two mash tubs, each hold 15,390 gallons. Backset is a fraction under 25 per cent. The water is heated to 100°F, then corn and rye are added. Taken to 210°F, held and then cooled with malt added at 152°F. Fermentation: 78 hours in 13 fermenters each holding 49,470 gallons. Beer still: 55 foot high, six foot wide. This takes spirit up to 125 proof. Copper doubler outside building increases it to 130 proof. The mashbill is principally in the 75/13/12 ration but for some brands a significantly higher use of rye is made.

JIM BEAM

Refuse to divulge details.

BERNHEIM

Corn from Indiana; rye from Minnesota; barley malt from Dakotas. Mashing water from city water, run through carbon beds to purify and remove chlorine. Backset is 12.5per cent. Cook up to 185°F, add corn, wheat/rye, then take up to 212°F for about 15 minutes. Allow to cool to 150°F to add malt. Fermentation: five 124,000 gallons fermenters. A further 12.5 per cent backset is added. Fermentation time: 72 hours. There are two five foot diameter stainless steel stills (the three sections at top are copper). Thumper (a type of doubler containing water, through which vapours from the beer still pass causing a distinctive thumping sound): stainless steel with copper at the bottom. The spirit leaves the stills at 140 proof, and is put through de-ionized water in the thumper to increase copper contact and strip out impurities.

EARLY TIMES

Corn from central Indiana; rye from Minnesota; barley malt from the Dakotas and Minnesota. Mashing water from city supply, after having previously been used in cooling process to burn off any chlorine. Using just 10 per cent backset, corn added at 155°F. This is taken up 240°F at pressure, held for fifteen minutes. Cooled down to 195°F to add rye slurry and cooled further to 152°F to add malt. Fermentation: twelve 42,000 gallons metal fermenters. Fermentation takes 3-7 days. Distilling: two 50 foot beer stills, one four

Left
Bubbling beer at
Maker's Mark –
a good distiller
can tell just how
long the mash
has been
fermenting by
the shape of the
bubbles.

and one five foot in diameter. Spirit emerges from the thumper at 140 proof. Reduced to 125 for barrelling (same process for Old Forester except using different yeast).

FOUR ROSES

Corn from Indiana; rye varies depending on quality but western Canadian is preferred and Swedish; barley malt from Minnesota. Mashing water from Salt River quarter mile east of distillery. Initial backset is 5 per cent. Corn dropped in cold, for premalt it goes up to 212°F, cooled to 160°F to add rye and down to 148°F for malt. This is held at 145°F for 15 minutes (whole process takes $3^1/_2$ hours, and is hot for just over an hour). Twenty-three fermenters hold 14,600 gallons each. Another 20 per cent backset is used in the fermenter. Fermentation time: 75-80 hours. Stills: 48 inch diameter, comes out at 130 proof doubled up to 138 proof. Reduced down to 120 proof. Heavy char on barrels.

LABROT AND GRAHAM

Corn from Kentucky; rye from Kentucky whenever possible or states further north; barley malt from Midwest. Water from 80 foot well in a limestone shelf, situated close to a dam downstream of the warehouses. Mashing: limestone water, 20 per cent backset stillage. Then heat to 140°F, add a pre-malt to help introduce grains into the water without it making doughballs. Add corn at 212°F. Hold for 20 minutes, reduce temp to 170°F. Add rye, hold 5-10 minutes cool to 150°F, add remaining malt. Cooks (mashes) on Thursday and Friday. The Thursday mash will be transferred to one of four 7,500 gallon cypress wood fermenters on same day. Fermentation will continue until Monday. Only part of the beer will be distilled that day, some will be distilled Tuesday and even possibly Wednesday. Likewise Friday mashes will be fermented until Thursday, Friday, Saturday. The temperature of the mash is set between 70-80°F depending on day. It is transferred over to the first (beer) still, where it is distilled to 40 proof. Then the second (high wine) still, where it is distilled to 110 proof. Then on to the third (spirit) still, where it is distilled up to 158 proof. It is reduced to 110 proof for the barrel.

MAKER'S MARK

Corn from local limestone belt, no further north than southern Indiana; winter wheat from within five miles of distillery, including that provided by catholic Sisters of Loretto; malt from Milwaukee, Wisconsin. Mashing water provided by small local spring-fed lake on hill a few hundreds yards west of distillery. Corn heated to 140°F then up to 212°F. Wheat is added at 156°F, malt at 148°F. Backset at around 25 per cent. Fermentation: further backset added to take it up to 32 per cent of mash. Yeast strain is the original from when distillery re-opened in 1954. Fermentation time: 3-4 days. Distilling: beer still (three foot diameter) takes it to 120 proof. It is then doubled to 130 proof. Reduced to 110 proof for barrelling. A three char barrel is used.

WILD TURKEY

Corn from Kentucky, Indiana; rye is mostly from Canada; barley malt six-row variety from Dakotas. Mashing water from Kentucky River and lake in Tyrone quarry. Heat to 140-160°F. Corn added then heated up to 212°F then cooled. Rye added at around 160°F then malt at 150°F. Fermentation: cooled down to 60°F, add own daily-made yeast (same yeast for at least 44 years). Fermenters of cypress wood and steel: nine at 30,000 and 16 at 16,000 gallons. Fermentation time 72-96 hours. Distilling: five foot diameter, (all copper), takes the spirit to just below 120 proof, then on to the doubler where strength is increased again.

TENNESSEE

JACK DANIEL

Corn from mid-west; rye and barley malt from Minnesota, Dakotas. Mashing water supplied from cave water (56°F all year). Corn goes in at 150°F heated up to 212°F, held for 15 minutes, cooled to 170°F then rye added. Cooled to 148°F for malt. Back set makes up 28 per cent.

Fermentation: 48 fermenters, all stainless steel, 40,000 gallon capacity each. No further backset. Fermentation time: 5-6 days. Stills: four of them, all copper, 54 inch diameter. Spirit comes out at 140 proof, passed through doubler used to strip impurities but does not carry out a second fermentation.

GEORGE DICKEL

Corn from mid-west; rye and malt from Dakotas. Mashing water Cascade spring (the cooling water is from the Cascade stream). Cook corn to 212°F, rye added when cooled to 180°F, malt added when cooled 146°F. Yeast: own specific strain. Backset: an initial 10 per cent into the mash, another 20 per cent later. Fermentation: 72-96 hours depending on whether running weekends. Still column: four foot diameter with 18 plates, all stainless steel. Doubler has copper pipe inside. Distills to 110 proof, doubles to 130 proof.

GEORGIA

VIKING

Corn and rye exclusively from Georgia. Water from well on the distillery site. Mashing: heat water to 115°F, add ground corn and rye and then add a pre-malt enzyme. Cook to 250°F then add same enzyme at 180°F to convert liquefied starch to sugar. Cooled down to 140°F, then enters heat exchanger to further cool to 76-78°F. Fermentation: six cypress, one copper and six stainless fermenters, totalling 124,000 gallons capacity. Backset used is 10 per cent. Distilling: beer still stainless steel with copper fillings at head. Single distillation to 135 proof, no doubler used. New oak barrels used.

INDIANA

SEAGRAM

Corn from Indiana; rye from Western Canada and Sweden; malted Barley from Minnesota. Water from underground wells rich in calcium carbonate. The corn and rye are mashed in together and cooked to 210°F, then cooled and malt added at 148°F, backset makes up 25 per cent. Fermentation in 14 cypress wood fermenters each holding 25,000 gallons. Fermentation time: in the region of 80 hours. Distillation is in four foot diameter all copper beer still distills up to 130 proof, doubled to 135 in copper doubler.

AN A-Z OF DISTILLERIES

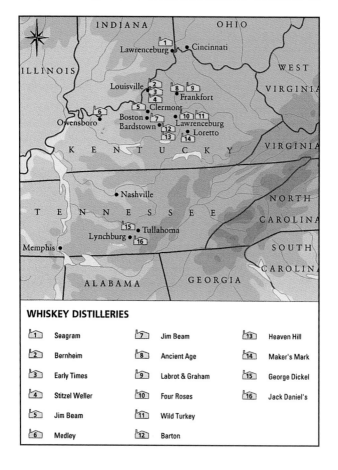

WHISKEY DISTILLERIES

1	Seagram	7	Jim Beam	13	Heaven Hill
2	Bernheim	8	Ancient Age	14	Maker's Mark
3	Early Times	9	Labrot & Graham	15	George Dickel
4	Stitzel Weller	10	Four Roses	16	Jack Daniel's
5	Jim Beam	11	Wild Turkey		
6	Medley	12	Barton		

BOURBON

ANCIENT AGE

A journey around America's bourbon distilleries should always begin in Kentucky's state capital, Frankfort, whether in the pages of a book or by car. So it is fitting that Ancient Age should crop up, alphabetically at least, as Kentucky's first distillery. By happy coincidence, the more of its whiskey I taste over the years, the more I wonder whether it is the leader in quality, too.

The town and environs of Frankfort were probably once amongst, per capita, the busiest distilling centres in Kentucky. Louisville, the state's largest city, will claim to have been ahead but situated as it is on the banks of the Ohio it became heavily populated very fast and though there were more distilleries, there were many other industries which offered employment to a swelling population.

Frankfort grew more sedately. It had become the state capital as early as 1783 and while the town expanded out of marshland with controlled elegance, distillers found spots nearby on the creeks feeding the Kentucky river which flows through the city, or on the Kentucky itself.

One of these distilleries was founded on a site which predated even Frankfort. That was Leestown, situated where buffalo once crossed the river in their thousands, attracting native American Indians, including the Cherokee, who knew where to feast on bounteous supplies of animals that slowed almost to a halt as they waited their turn to cross. Here Daniel Boone is said to have encountered a fishing Indian, dispatching him before reinforcements were called.

It was also a spot that later, in 1775, surveyor and explorer Captain Willis Lee recognised for its potential for starting a community that might thrive on river business. One of his team enthused: "A richer and more beautiful country than this I have not seen in all America. We have laid up a town seventy miles up ye Kentucke where I intend to live, and I don't doubt that there will be fifty families living in it by Christmas." The traveller Nicholas Cresswell recalled that year on meeting Lee, who was to be killed by Indians: "[Lee] treated me very kindly with a dram of whiskey." Whether it was from the very first batch ever distilled in Leestown or from provisions, sadly, he did not say. Leestown did flourish for a short while but just a very short distance up river another crossing became even better known. It was called Frank's Ford, named

after Stephen Frank, a member of a party of
settlers who was killed when Indians attacked
while they slept at an overnight camp they had
made on the eastern shore of the Kentucky. When
a town began to grow there too, it became known
as Frankfort. In 1777 Leestown was temporarily
abandoned after an Indian attack and although it
was repopulated, it fell into slow and terminal
decline. Today it is not even granted a place-name
on the most detailed map.

The site of the Ancient Age distillery is just yards
from where tobacco, hemp and whiskey were sent
down the Kentucky river to markets in New
Orleans. The first distillery arrived much later and
from a rather unexpected source. Benjamin
Blanton had left Kentucky to join other
prospectors in the 1849 gold rush. His journey was
not a fruitless one and he returned to Kentucky a
wealthy man. With his proceeds he bought Rock
Hill Farm close to the Leestown site and after some
minor distilling there decided in 1865 to go full
tilt. He built a distillery where the present one
proudly stands today. He owned it for only four
years before he sold it on to a Richard Tobin.

It became known as the OFC Distillery, short
for Old Fire Copper and OFC became a famous
brand around Kentucky and beyond for many
years. In the early 1870s the distillery became
part of the Edmund Taylor empire. (He had also
bought Labrot and Graham at this time and
during the period of 1873-4 made improvements

to both distilleries.)

Indeed, one of the most endearing aspects of the present Ancient Age distillery is the way in which the buildings seem to take in a wide spectrum of styles perfectly representing the architecture of their time. No other Kentucky distillery offers so much to the industrial archaeologist, because the story did not end with Taylor. He sold the distillery on to George T. Stagg, who had also owned Labrot and Graham, and from then on it became known as the Old Stagg distillery. As well as its famous whiskey, OFC, the Taylor brand was one they also continued to make.

At one point there were even two distilleries working side by side. George Dickel had needed

Above

The visitor's centre at the Ancient Age distillery near Leestown by the Kentucky river.

to escape Tennessee as Prohibition moved in ahead of the national blanket ban. So they set up their stills first at Louisville and then, during World War II when Stagg became part of the giant Schenley distillers, who also owned Dickel, with the Stagg complex. To make Dickel's Cascade whiskey, special Tennessee-style carbon filters had to be employed. The distillery building still stands today, redundant since Dickel returned safely home to a new purpose-built plant.

Today most of the brands are under Japanese control. In 1986 the Takara Shuzo company was the first to buy a Scottish distillery, Tomatin, outright. Since then they briefly added the Leestown Distilling Company to their portfolio, before selling it off to Sazerac, but keeping the brands. Yet despite all these changes one truly remarkable fact remains which possibly helps explain why Ancient Age whiskey is without doubt in the top three or four you can find anywhere in the world today. Since 1912 there have been only five distillery managers. The first was Colonel Albert Blanton, son of the distillery's founder. He started there in 1897 as a 16-year-old office boy when it had already become the Stagg distillery. Fifteen years later he was promoted to distillery manager, retiring in 1952 by which time he was vice-president of Schenley. He taught much of what he knew to Elmer T. Lee, manager from 1969-80. And now Joe Darmond is in control while Gary Gayheart

Left
The statue of
Colonel Albert
Blanton,
distillery
manager for over
50 years, watches
over the Ancient
Age distillery.

carries on where Elmer left off as master distiller.

Yet even now, Elmer still has a say in at least one of the company's brands. Despite having been officially retired for nearly 18 years, he still slips into the plant each Monday (and a few other days besides) and selects casks from Warehouse H for Blanton's and wanders around the other warehouses on the lookout for an exceptional cask which will go into the supreme

Elmer T. Lee bourbon, one of only three whiskies named after distillers still living. Gary's responsibility is selecting casks for the masterful Hancock's Reserve. Ancient Age have been leading the way for some time now with single barrel bottlings and slowly, and not before time, the world is waking up to just what a wonderful distillery this is.

The distillery itself is huge: no little Maker's Mark and Labrot and Graham, this. Built to slake the thirst of a nation, the fact that they can do so and make good whiskey into the bargain is a wonderful added bonus. The fermenters are almost unreal in size: 12 copper-alloy fermenters, each holding 90,000 gallons (that's twelve times the capacity of nearest neighbour L&G whose wooden fermenters hold a minuscule 7,500 gallons each). And the stills are equally enormous, looking from the bottom as if they had been installed by NASA.

Ancient Age, with its eerie statue of Colonel Blanton overlooking the beautifully manicured grounds and the garish red and white water tower allowing you to pinpoint its location from afar, is some distillery and one still hiding its light under a bushel. But you cannot help believing that as soon as it is discovered by the whiskey-drinking world, tourists will come flocking like the buffalo that once blazed a trail to this very same spot.

ANCIENT AGE • 4-YEAR-OLD • 90 PROOF

NOSE A sexy, intense nose teeming with all kinds of complexity. The small grains are quite big here with rye and malt easily identified. But the secret lies in the interlinking fruits, like raisins and there is a similar style to the better notes of well-matured eastern European plum brandy. Truly superb.

TASTE Big, complicated start with much more toast and cereal than the 80 proof version. More corn oil, less nuttiness and a build-up of rye for the middle.

FINISH The bitter cocoa returns for the finale with great confidence. There are also some fresh dates and raisins to add balance and weight and some bigger oaky notes to give that unmissable bourbon characteristic.

COMMENTS For a 4-year-old this bourbon shows enormous power and character. Beyond the alcohol there is extra weight on the oak which guarantees a bigger presence in the mouth.

This 4-year-old also comes at 80 and 100 proof. The 80 proof is just a tad too light for this age as occasional lack of complexity is made too plain to see. The 100 proof can sometimes be a little too severe if the whiskey hasn't quite hit balance. But this is nitpicking. Both are usually superb, but the 90 proof above does seem to have the perfect weight.

ANCIENT AGE BARREL 107
10 YEAR OLD • 107 PROOF

A fruitier, more oak intense version of the AAA 10-year-old, though oddly enough for a whiskey of this strength, nothing quite so long and delightful. Still, another strapping whiskey of enormous character and delight.

ANCIENT AGE
38 MONTHS • 80 PROOF

This is the weakest of all the distillery's brands. Very green, thin and citrusy and off-key from start to finish. Designed for ice and water only.

ANCIENT ANCIENT AGE
10-YEAR-OLD • 86 PROOF

NOSE This is easily one of the most complex aromas of any straight, single-aged whiskey in the world. Despite a spicy prickle on the nose those softer toffee notes form the perfect background to hints of orange peel, echoes of unidentifiable herbs, salt, honey, leather and oak. Each time you nose it the character has changed just a shade. And each bottle you nose has these same properties but with one always slightly more dominant than the other. This one has orange peel. Another I have has slightly more honey. Once I picked out basil quite clearly. Other times it is lost in a garden of other herbs. Intriguing and magnificent.

TASTE Just a little drier at first than the nose suggests with that salty, oaky, slightly mouth-puckering feel hitting home first. Then it becomes lip-smacking as these notes stay but are joined by oily toffee notes and very rich cocoa.

FINISH Amazingly long and there is an increase in the spice. The cocoa hangs on for ever with some vanilla and oak keeping it good company.

COMMENTS This is mesmeric stuff. It is quite a dry bourbon, really. But there is just the right toffee presence to form a perfect balance. This is the whiskey I ask for first when in Kentucky and in search of something with a character and class of its own.

ANCIENT AGE 10 STAR • 6-YEAR-OLD • 90 PROOF

NOSE Lively and even a little hot with green, ripe, juicy apples and toffee.

TASTE Very creamy, even oily start then a quick burst of peppers. These slowly fade to leave delightful toffee core with vanilla.

FINISH Much drier with the vanilla taking an early grip. Some very dark, bitter chocolate has an important say on the finish.

COMMENTS Not quite as in tune as the better 4-year-olds though some complexity, if not quite perfectly formed, has begun to start working its magic.

BENCHMARK 94 PROOF
Another great whiskey from a great distillery. Really mouth-filling bourbon which switches brilliantly from sweet to dry.

BLANTON'S • 93 PROOF
A 6-8-year-old that can sometimes be honey-sweet when at 6/7 and a little drier and chewier when a year older.

NOSE Unmistakable Ancient Age: just a hint of salt touches off the leather and molasses sweetness. Deep and very satisfying.

TASTE A masterful start with powerful dry vanilla notes in perfect harmony with hints of honey amid the strong caramel.

FINISH Long, creamy caramel holds the fort until some late soft peppers arrive to spice things up.

COMMENTS The underlying dryness amid the spice and honey really makes for a bourbon that should suit all tastes and one to keep the discerning whiskey drinker almost purring with delight.

BLANTON'S • (8-YEAR-OLD UNSTATED)
93 PROOF
(Gold waxed and gold/brown print.)

Japan only. Discreetly weightier than the average Blanton; lusher, creamier, fatter with excellent corn and rye richness and then caramel and spice. This is a masterful whiskey, a classic amongst classics.

BLANTON'S BLACK • 80 PROOF
(Black labelled.)

Japan only. Misses the intensity of the stronger Blanton's, which underlines just what this whiskey is all about. The balance is also lacking just a little.

BLANTON'S GOLD EDITION • 103 PROOF

(Gold embossed writing; gold as opposed to brass horse and jockey stopper, claret wax. Warehouse H Rick No. 6. Barrel No. 8. Dumped 24 February 1997.)

NOSE Fabulous. Honey and banana, deep corn and fruity, succulent rye gives extra weight. Some wood smoke, cloves and polished leather reveal its age.

TASTE Perfectly balanced honey sweetness and smoky, oaky tones are rounded off by a supreme, oily-textured mouthfeel which clings to the mouth.

FINISH Soft liquorice-tannins fight through honey and slightly sherried fruitiness. Very, very long.

COMMENTS This is probably one of the finest whiskies you are likely to taste anywhere in the world. Very few are so supremely balanced, although it is lacking its usual spiciness. Truly glorious, none the less.

EAGLE RARE • 10-YEAR-OLD • 101 PROOF

Impressive stuff, but not really up to usual, subtle Ancient Age standards. Just a little too roasty and rich.

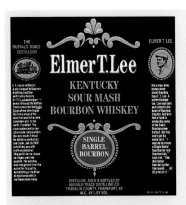

ELMER T. LEE SINGLE BARREL BOURBON
90 PROOF

Originally, Elmer T. Lee's name was given to a bourbon vatted from a number of barrels. Many bottles of this can still be found around the world, but now in single barrel form only, and still each individually selected by now retired master distiller Elmer T. Lee. The label says Buffalo Trace Distilling Company. There is no age mentioned on the label as Elmer picks each barrel not because of how old it is but how the bourbon has progressed in the barrel. For that reason it may vary between 6 and 8 years. This sample, at a guess, is around 7, nudging 8.

NOSE Something of a cross in intensity between the standard Blanton's and the older Japanese version. Rich malt and lively rye plus cumquats and mint - even a hint of juniper. Quite toasty, too.

TASTE Just where do you begin to describe...? Quite fat and chewy with early honey sweetness and raisins. Some cocoa adds extra depth to the vanilla.

FINISH
Extremely long, and then at last begins to dry with a return of juniper and more cocoa.

COMMENTS

I have never had an Elmer T. Lee which has been less than stunning. This one just fails to end. A bourbon of beguiling and astonishing complexity which achieves the seemingly impossible: it actually outshines the Blanton's.

HANCOCK'S RESERVE • 88.9 PROOF

NOSE Oily and fat with cream toffee and very lightly spiced oaky tones. A little sweeter than one expects from this distillery, though just as enticing.

TASTE A sweet body to start off with and lots of chewable cream caramel. The vanilla arrives pretty early but the mouth feel remains fat and glorious.

FINISH Dries out very quickly as the oak does have an important part to play. The caramel hangs on throughout.

COMMENTS This is an immensely enjoyable bourbon with the whole always being a lot more complex and lip-smacking than the sum of its parts.

BARTON

Some distilleries were put on this planet to make whiskey and eschew all the other stuff about aesthetics, romance and history. Well, this is Kentucky's representative.

Which is all rather odd, considering that this was the home distillery of Oscar Getz, the first man to try and put bourbon on the map by setting up a museum, initially within the plant and then more elegantly and elaborately at Stamford Hall in downtown Bardstown.

The distillery in its present entirely utilitarian form dates back to 1946 and there is little or no trace of the famous old Tom Moore Distillery that occupied the site from the late 1880s. This was the same Tom Moore of Mattingley and Moore fame, one of the most popular whiskies of its day. Perhaps the only visible link with the past is the lake which feeds the distillery, Teurs Lake. Fed by limestone springs, it was named after Harry Teur who bought the distillery at the end of Prohibition. And it was he who began the modernisation programme, though it was the new owner Oscar Getz who made the plant the most modern of its time.

The construction includes outdoor fermenters, which saves money on building walls and a roof

Above
The vast distilling enterprise at Barton extends over some 180 acres.

to house them. And everything is steel. Even the massive stills, which concede to copper only in the heads. The one piece of apparatus that is proudly all copper, the doubler, is located on the outside of the building but heavily lagged.

The whiskey made at Barton's, though, does not seem to suffer, although one or two brands, especially Colonel Lee leave much to be desired. The general house style is busy on the palate with lots of small grains, though the oldest whiskey, Very Old Barton, is just six years old. The brand I like best of all, Kentucky Gentleman, has loads of rye character and this is probably helped not only by the fact that a mashbill with a significantly higher rye content is favoured (something I believe to be in the region of 60 per cent corn to 30 per cent rye and 10 per cent malt, as opposed to a standard 74/16/10), but the distillery carries out the unusual practice of adding the rye to the corn during the cooking process, thereby extracting every last bit of flavour from that hardy and fruity grain. With each tasting your respect for master distiller Bill Friel's skills increases as the whiskey has an alarming habit of growing on you. Sadly, as hard as you try, the same can't be said for the distillery.

BARCLAY'S BOURBON 80 PROOF

NOSE Slightly astringent vanilla, spirity and harsh. Yet unmistakably a bourbon for all that, and of the old-fashioned kind.

TASTE Firm corn in the custardy sweet, attractive start. The vanilla sits attractively in the middle.

FINISH A sweetish, nut-oil finish. Then, as the oak arrives, it becomes more bitter. Perhaps too short and becomes rather corny and hard at the very death with not quite enough oak.

COMMENTS I quite like this one though not one I'd particularly go in search of. Non-pretentious, non-sophisticated yet attractive for its simplicity. Let down only by its rather miserly finish.

COLONEL LEE
80 AND 100 PROOF

The nose is raw and unsophisticated. Fiery and bitter, this makes a single-handed assault for the title of the worst bourbon on the market. Genuinely hard to find a good word about it.

KENTUCKY GENTLEMAN BIB • 100 PROOF

NOSE Despite the strength, or maybe because of it, this is the least creative nose of the brand in any of its three strengths. A little malt hangs on the alcohol but that is all.

TASTE The full enormity of this whiskey arrives with a sweet, explosive blast. The small grains are extremely active, constantly pricking at the taste-buds with the oily caramel trying to act as a restraint. Lots of rye meets the middle as it becomes drier and a little fruitier.

FINISH Long, dry, oaky finish. Bigger than one might expect from a whiskey this age. The vanillas hang on but hardly sweeten at all.

COMMENTS Few bourbons, it has to be said, have so much to say at so young an age (four years old). Not the kind of whiskey to slink back into your chair with after a hard day. More one to get you back on your feet. Great stuff. Also available and extremely impressive at 80 and 86 proof, though the 100 has the edge.

TEN HIGH • 80 PROOF

Once Ten High was a medium hefty bourbon made by Barton for the Walker label. This, though, is an insipid, rather uninteresting shadow of its former self.

TOM MOORE • 80 PROOF

NOSE A fine medium to rare nose: the tell-tale vanilla-oakiness of bourbon is there but never overdone. There is also some fruit, like boiled gooseberries and blackcurrant.

TASTE Lots and lots of cream toffee underlines this bourbon's desire to stay mid-range. Although quite sweet, a little like sugared milk, there is a rye hardness and bitterness which helps make for a mouth-filling middle.

FINISH A little cinnamon and ginger arrive towards the end though the cream toffee keeps on going.

COMMENTS This is a charming bourbon, not in any way heavy or challenging but just simple and easy-going. A wonderful example of an old-fashioned style of Kentucky bourbon which old-timers remember as being quite prevalent in the 1950s. Also available as a BIB 100 proof version: and though very drinkable, it does not possess quite the same charm.

VERY OLD BARTON
6-YEAR-OLD • 80 PROOF

NOSE Hints of Ceylon tea amid salty olives show what an extra couple of years in the cask can achieve for a Kentucky bourbon. Very deep, but in the Barton house style, never remotely heavy, either. There is a little waxiness, too.

TASTE A silky start on the palate with sweet corn dominating as the usual toffee one expects from this distillery arrives in style.

FINISH Much more rye noticeable and then a drying hardness.

COMMENTS There is a lot going on, but it never becomes a complex whiskey. Even so, a highly enjoyable, immensely mouth-filling bourbon just a notch up in weight and depth by comparison with its stable mates all round. With Kentucky Gentleman the VOB brands represent the pick of the Barton portfolio. VOB is also available at 86 and 90 proof.

VERY OLD BARTON BIB • 100 PROOF

NOSE The rye kicks in early here and some malt can be picked up, too. Hints of mango and melon give an unexpected fruitiness.

TASTE Much crisper start with the rye following on confidently from the nose. Still sweet but with a bigger corn oil character than the other VOBs.

FINISH One of the more complex of the Barton range. The small grains help form quite a peppery attack with the vanilla also being much sharper in character.

COMMENTS A genuine mouthful markedly different from the other VOBs. I have been told that anything carrying the VOB label has to be 6 years old. But I'm not convinced about this at all. The superb small grains flit around in a similar fashion to the 4-year-old Old Crow from Beam. This seems younger to me. And there is no age statement on the label. The plot thickens.

JIM BEAM

Opposite
Jim Beam is the
only whiskey in
the world
available on
draft and that's
only if your
local is Chicago's
Twisted Spoke.

There is a superb bar in Chicago, the Twisted Spoke, where you can ask for Jim Beam on draught. And what's more you will get it. It is the only whiskey I know to be on tap anywhere in the world. Not surprising really as Jim Beam is very much in demand: it is the biggest-selling bourbon brand by a mile.

Perhaps for that reason it is sniffed at by the purists (and not just to get the scent of the glass). Certainly the odd mouthful I have had over the years has been flat and uninspiring, but that has certainly been the exception rather than the rule. In many pubs, bars and restaurants the world over Beam has long been seen flying the flag for bourbon just as Glenfiddich does for single malt scotch.

And just like Glenfiddich, the standard bottling of Beam tells only a fraction of the story about what their whiskey is all about. Glenfiddich still needs another six or eight years in the cask before it starts unfurling its true colours; Beam, thanks to the warmer Kentucky climes, needs perhaps only half that time. And then we are talking a very impressive whiskey, indeed.

The American whiskey industry without the Beam family would be like a Kentucky garden

without a Red Cardinal. As well as founding and still being involved in the most famous bourbon distillery of them all, you will find Beams also at Heaven Hill and Jack Daniels. And it was they who got the Early Times distillery going. Since World War II they have even popped up in Pennsylvania.

You have to go a long way back into Kentucky history to find the first Beam distiller. The man who started it all was a German by the name of Jacob Boehm who embarked upon a new life in America during the mid-18th century and arrived in Kentucky via Maryland and Pennsylvania, two major rye whiskey producing areas. Now this is where things get confusing. According to a copy of a 100-year-old newspaper article I have from Nelson County, where the Beam distillery is situated, Jacob began distilling in 1788, a year or two after he settled in Kentucky. That makes sense. What is odd is that Jim Beam claimed that he didn't sell his first barrel until 1795, and in 1995 the 200th anniversary of Jim Beam was celebrated with some gusto. So it's the seven intervening years that are a mystery: nobody at that time matured their whiskey seven years before selling it! And in those very hard times it is extraordinary to think that he would not have sold as much as he could, or at least bartered.

What is beyond dispute is that Jacob had two sons, David and John. While John went forth to beget Early Times, David stayed at home and tended the family business, and it was while under his auspices that it became known as the Old Tub distillery. Marketing the Old Tub brand (rather than a Beam brand – that was carried out by John at Early Times) he carried on until the 1890s when his son Jim Beam and his son-in-law took over the distillery and renamed it the Beam and Hart Old Tub Distillery. The distillery closed during Prohibition but was back in action once the government came to its senses. This time Jim, at 70 years of age and with the desire to make whiskey still coursing through his veins, was back in harness with his son Jeremiah

But after some 150 years the business went out of the family's hands when it was sold off during World War II to one of their best suppliers, Blum of Chicago, who had already become a partner in the company. For the last 30 years Jim Beam has

Opposite
Barrels of Jim Beam maturing up in the buzzard roost of a warehouse at their Boston distillery.

been owned by American Brands, but a Beam has always been on hand to continue distilling there. In fact there is usually any number of Beams. Carl and Baker Beam have been master distillers in their time and Jim Beam's grandson, Booker Noe, master distiller emeritus, is today the distillery's figurehead, a larger than life character who with Baker shares the distinction of having whiskies named after them. One of his sons works there even now.

Jim Beam have two distilleries. The most famous, Clermont, is actually nearer Bardstown, or even Louisville, than it is to Frankfort, which is the address on every Beam label. The second distillery is at Boston and is seldom mentioned. Yet for me it makes the better whiskey of the two.

In recent years the Clermont distillery has set up a tourist attraction, the Jim Beam American Outpost. And it goes without saying that the location of the distillery is particularly impressive. It sits in typically Kentucky terrain, the land undulating and pleasing to the eye. Across the road from the distillery is an edge of the beautiful Bernheim Forest, given to the commonwealth by Louisville distiller Ike Bernheim.

But because the distillery has to produce the world's most coveted bourbon, plus major US brands like Old Taylor, Old Crow and Old Grand-Dad to boot, it is not surprising to find that the inside of the distillery is not a Wild Turkey or a Maker's Mark. Instead the place is

geared to efficiency. The washbacks are stainless steel and the amount of copper in the beer stills is negligible to save wear and tear. But that said, after a few years in the barrel the whiskey does start polishing up nicely.

Over at Boston, to the south of the forest but still in Nelson County, there is no evidence of the hubbub that Clermont attracts. Here they go about making their whiskey quietly, to the same specifications used in the portfolio of Jim Beam brands. The inside is a bit more cramped and has a more lived-in look than Clermont. But the spirit that gushes from the stills is a little richer, fuller, fatter and spicier. It just goes to prove that you cannot make exactly the same whiskey in two different places, no matter how you try.

Above
The workaday Boston plant, while not as pretty as its sister in Clermont, on balance distils the more charming whiskey of the two.

**BEAM'S CHOICE • 5-YEAR-OLD (UNSTATED)
80 PROOF**

NOSE Sexy, fruity nose. Stunningly enticing simply because everything is so laid back and delicate. An understated nose of toffee-raisin, apple and a hint of raspberry.

TASTE Soft and silky mouth-entry immediately jazzes up as some oak-induced spice arrives. No real fruit (except for a hint of apple, maybe) on the palate despite the nose, but weighty liquorice arrives to claim the middle ground.

FINISH More spice, like very faint peppers, bounce around for a while; the liquorice fades and a cleaner more corn-assertive and vaguely oaky theme continues to the very end.

COMMENTS There may only be six months to a year in difference between standard Jim Beam and Beam's Choice but the difference in style is extraordinary. Any wild notes which may occasionally get through on the younger version are eradicated as Beam's Choice majestically eases its way from nose to finish: never particularly complex, it just tastes real good.

JIM BEAM • 80 PROOF

NOSE Extremely light and delicate, a very slight sulphury note can occasionally tweak the nose buds, but overall corn-sweet and attractive with very soft vanilla.

TASTE Big vanilla and toffee are the main attributes here, but it does remain dry and full throughout. With a very attractive corn-rich middle.

FINISH For such a delicate bourbon the finish is both surprisingly long and complex. There may be some oakiness creeping in, and a little touch of spice, too. Excellent ebbing and flowing of those toffee notes continues for some time.

COMMENTS Not quite as floral on the nose as 5 years to a decade ago. And like all delicate whiskies the world over, there can be slight variance of weight from bottle to bottle. But for something criticised for being "mass produced", standard Jim Beam is a delightful bourbon with a gentle, more-ish and quite engaging personality.

JIM BEAM BLACK LABEL • 8-YEAR-OLD • 90 PROOF

NOSE
Firm, sweet vanilla and a distinctive menthol, slightly minty, note paints an entirely different Jim Beam picture from anything else.

TASTE
Excellent mouth-feel and immediate feeling of heftiness from the oak. A sturdy, sweet liquorice middle becomes quite oily and clingy.

FINISH
Long, long finish thanks to those oils which cling limpet-like to the roof of the mouth. A first-rate sweetness maintains its presence for some considerable time while a hickory, salt and slightly burnt toast presence builds up for the grand finale. Very soft throughout.

COMMENTS
This brand has improved over the years, being nothing like as spirity as of old. Consequently its full body is given full rein. Luscious and delightfully sweet from the moment it enters the mouth. A fine, highly complex bourbon and about the heaviest American style outside Jack Daniels which enjoys a similar character.

JIM BEAM GOLD LABEL • 8-YEAR-OLD 100 PROOF

Same age as Black Label but an altogether different slant with more honey on nose and crisper taste and liquorice and honey on the finish. Excellent, delicate stuff.

JIM BEAM SEVEN-YEAR-OLD

Apart from a subtle 7 years on the label, almost indistinguishable from the standard 4-year-old. Until you nose and taste it. This is more smoky and oily to nose with corresponding fatness to taste. Much more corn dominance than normal. Pleasant but less spicy and complex.

BAKER'S • 7-YEAR-OLD • 107 PROOF

Another first class bourbon with plenty of oily, lingering character. Those mixed spices blend superbly with the toffee and touches of honey. Beautiful.

BASIL HAYDEN'S

Kentucky Straight
Bourbon Whiskey

WHEN BASIL HAYDEN, SR. began distilling his smooth BOURBON here in 1796, KENTUCKY was but four years old and GEORGE WASHINGTON was PRESIDENT.

Today, we make BASIL HAYDEN'S Kentucky Straight Bourbon WHISKEY using the same skill and care that made it a favorite among AMERICA'S frontier settlers.

DISTILLED AND BOTTLED BY
KENTUCKY SPRINGS DISTILLING CO.
CLERMONT · FRANKFORT, KENTUCKY USA
750 ML
40% ALC./VOL. (80 PROOF)

BASIL HAYDEN'S
8-YEAR-OLD • 80 PROOF

Magical and mercurial, this is one of Kentucky's most gentle noses yet boasts wonderful riches. Dry and pleasantly oaky. At the very end it sweetens out into cream toffee rather like a high class Canadian.
A lovely bourbon: a gentleman of a whiskey. Every note is understated, almost ethereal. Delicious.

BOOKER'S • 92 MONTHS
126.1 PROOF

NOSE As heavy and threatening as a Kentucky summer's evening before a storm. Lots of deep vanilla and honey. Sometimes it's fruity, too, with mango or blueberry.

TASTE Gloriously velvety as it enters the mouth, viscous and palate filling. Immediately oak-intense with fat liquorice and caramel.

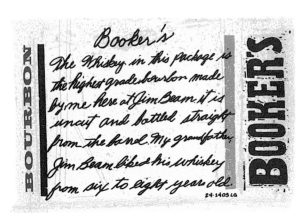

Booker's
The Whiskey in this package is
the highest grade bourbon made
by me here at Jim Beam. It is
uncut and bottled straight
from the barrel. My grandfather
Jim Beam liked his whiskey
from six to eight year old.
24-1405 LG

FINISH Amazingly long, lightens and sweetens all the time until it hits cream toffee mode before there is a late upsurge of dry oak. Very faint spice at the death.

COMMENTS Booker Noe is a big man and a great name in whiskey. I guess the same can be said about this brand. Even its nut brown colour takes the breath away. Few whiskies enjoy such a luxuriant arrival on the palate and then manage to achieve such intensity afterwards. In that respect, it has the hallmarks of a heavy-peated Islay Scotch single malt. And following in certain Scottish distillers' footsteps the whiskey has been improved by being put into bottle un-cut with water and un-chill filtered straight from the cask. Impressive, imperious and hugely enjoyable.

BOURBON DE LUXE • 80 PROOF

NOSE Heavyweight rye makes a surprising entrance. Few standard 4-year-olds have so much rye character and it is ably assisted by soft toffee vanilla. Despite this, is just a little fresh and young.

TASTE Surging rye hits the palate running. The taste-buds are swamped with so much character and the sweetness builds up slowly as does the oiliness. Excellent mouth-feel and genuinely smooth.

FINISH Some corn lightness is at last allowed in but the rye firmness clings to the roof of the mouth. A little malt barley is also detectable before the toffee vanilla hinted on the nose takes hold.

COMMENTS A hugely enjoyable whiskey. For a 4-year-old it shows remarkable complexity and though still quite young holds up very well. The real treat, though, is the enormous rye character. Great stuff.

JACOB'S WELL • 7-YEAR-OLD • 84 PROOF

Named after Jacob Boehm who in 1788 began distilling whiskey and the Beam empire. A very pleasant whiskey that is genuinely mellow. Rather unsophisticated on the palate, this a lazy kind of bourbon that ambles over the taste-buds.

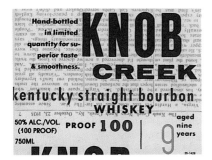

KNOB CREEK • 9-YEAR-OLD • 100 PROOF

NOSE More oak here than most Jim Beam brands, but this has a beautiful cinnamon and apple aroma to freshen it up. Also some hot brown sugar, too: a nose for someone with a sweet tooth!

TASTE From a sweet beginning, an even sweeter middle grows. The oak builds up in intensity, but there is a lovely peppercorn spice to act as a perfect counterweight.

FINISH A brittle rye hardness battles through and the sweetness becomes more focused. Medium length, the oak does not hang around too long. Yes there is vanilla but it is the small grain, especially the rye, which has by far the biggest say.

COMMENTS Like Booker's this has followed the Maker's Mark plastic-wax school of bottle sealing. Yet this a very different bourbon from any I know. I can think of only two or three others which are so compartmentalised as they work over the taste-buds. Yet despite its many facets it works really well to give you a bourbon of great complexity which just keeps you guessing in which direction it is going next. For its balance, versatility and downright magnificence this is probably my favourite creation from Jim Beam's two distilleries.

OLD CROW

For a century and a half the name Crow has been synonymous with good bourbon. The label on the present bottling incorrectly claims that James Crow actually invented sour mash whiskey. As we have seen earlier in the history of American whiskey, whiskey-distilling books published around 1818 already discussed that procedure. Crow did not enter the American whiskey industry for another five years. Educated in Edinburgh (the city which today produces Scotland's distillers) as a physician, Crow emigrated to America with his brother to set up business, but together they went bankrupt. Destitute, in 1823 he headed west alone and it was after walking the 50 miles from Louisville to Frankfort that he met Colonel Willis Field, a distiller. Field soon recognised Crow's potential and set him to work at his small distillery in Grier's Creek near Woodford County. There, Crow used his training in science (chemistry in particular) to set certain standards throughout all distilling procedures. To say he was the first to use hydrometers and other instruments as is so often claimed would be incorrect. But what Crow did achieve was teaching their correct use to the industry, as well as how the use of sour mash should differ according to certain circumstances. He also set up what was probably the first laboratory at any distillery in an old log cabin where he also lived. Until Crow's arrival

JAMES CROW, A NEW KIND OF PIONEER, ARRIVES IN KENTUCKY

A physician and chemist by training, James Crow reached Kentucky in 1825 and within a decade had revolutionized the making of Kentucky whiskey.

every distillery made an inconsistent spirit; under Crow, Field's whiskey became famed for its consistently high quality.

Crow eventually came to reside in Millville on Glenns Creek, five miles south of Frankfort, and it was while there that his fame grew. For 20 years he superintended the Labrot and Graham Distillery and later worked at the Johnson distillery, the site of which is now the Old Taylor

distillery on Glenns Creek. He died there in 1856, aged 67.

From newspaper accounts of Crow written during the 1870s and 1890s it was obvious that not only was he well respected as a distiller but also as a doctor. He was known never to charge for his ministrations to the local sick and to "walk for miles to bleed a patient". There is also a remarkable story (albeit with conflicting versions) regarding his wife. Some reports claim that he married while a successful businessman in New York. Another tells of his wife Eliza and daughter Catherine arriving from Scotland unannounced having spent years searching for him. As the tale goes, they had completely lost touch with James and only succeeded in tracing him to Glenns Creek on account of their hearing of a barrel with his name that was shipped to Scotland. It could have been that ashamed of his bankruptcy, he could not face his family again. With James a stout Presbyterian who kept his own council and never discussed his personal affairs, no one ever really got to the bottom of the story. Whatever, he never again left his family to whom he was obviously devoted. But there is one thing beyond doubt. Despite keeping company with Kentucky's foremost intellectuals and making a fortune for the distillers he worked for, especially the Peppers, he never did own a distillery of his own, despite his name being probably the most famous in the business at the

Opposite

Glenns Creek, five miles south of Frankfort and home of the Old Crow distillery.

97

time, and he died almost as penniless as when he arrived in Woodford County.

The enormous Old Crow distillery which sits on Glenns Creek today, just a mile from its confluence with the Kentucky, was built a decade after James' death. It continued in operation until 1987 when its then parent company National Distillers were taken over by Jim Beam. Until Prohibition the distillery continued to operate copper pot stills: four beer stills, at 3331, 3489, 3819 and 5182 gallons each and three spirit ones, two holding 950 gallons and the third 1200. In 1904 Van Johnson, a descendant of Crow's old employer Anderson Johnson, and distiller at the Old Crow plant from 1872 to 1903, explained in a legal document how Crow made his whiskey, having been given the recipe by William Mitchell who had worked alongside the famous doctor.

Use in 100 bushels of bourbon mash: corn 75% –80%, rye 8%–10%, barley malt 12–15%. In starting up the distillery and using small tubs put say 80lbs of corn meal in the tub and cook with say 30 to 40 gallons of boiling water. Let set for 4 to 5 hours, then stir and cool to 150–160 F., then add rye, say 8 to 10 lbs. Then cool down by stirring to 135–148 and then add malt, say 12 to 15 lbs. Then cool down to 115 F and add cold water enough to bring it down to 68–78 according to the temperature of the weather. Then fill the fermenter with water at same setting, temperature, then add yeast which has been made, say one and a half to three and a half lbs. to the bushel.

Continue the above for four days and thereafter cook the corn meal with boiling slop, then let stand for 12 to 24 hours, then break up and cool by stirring to 122–160. Then add rye, same percent as above, and cool to 120–130. Then add malt and hold for 2 hours. Then break up, run to fermenters and fill with water, or part water and part slop, at temperature of 68–78 according to the weather, and add either fresh yeast, or yeast taken from the previous tubs. The tubs for the first three days of the week are set at say 72–78, and the last 3 days say at 66–72.

Then run the beer into the stills, copper preferred and boil until the spirit is practically exhausted. Then run this spirit obtained from the first distillation, and which is held in tubs for the purpose, into the copper doubler and there boil until the whiskey is so made and would show about proof in the receiving room. The remainder being boiled until the whiskey is practically exhausted and which after cutting off is run into the low wine tub and distilled over again.

Yeast. Use proper proportions of rye, say one and half pounds, to the bushel, and cook same in 15 to 20 gallons of water to a temperature of say 160 to 175 for say 10 to 20 minutes; then follow with barley malt, same per cent, and let stand 24 hours at least to sour and cool to 70–76 degrees. Then stock it with jug yeast previously prepared.

That is how old Jim Crow is said to have made his whiskey, and there is not a single distiller in Kentucky who would not be able to follow that procedure today, except they would be probably be using continuous rather than old copper pots. And the "doubler" mentioned would be what in Scotland, and at Labrot and Graham, would be known as the spirit still. Classic bourbon, indeed.

Sadly, the whiskey under the name of Old Crow now is a rather feeble effort. It is a three-year-old of very little character. This is a shame because until 1997 Old Crow was a lovely four-year-old with a superb, refreshing spiciness which made it, with Ancient Age ten-year-old, my preferred everyday bourbon when in Kentucky.

I just hope the next time Jim Beam bring out a super premier bourbon, they keep the name Jim Crow and what he stood for in mind.

OLD CROW • 80 PROOF
(Look for bottlings that do not carry the 3-year-old age statement.)

NOSE Excellent complexity as the powerful malt, backed by citrus fruity (grapefruit?) rye, enjoys the company of a gentle spiciness. One of the most small-grain-dominant of all bourbon noses. An absolute treat.

TASTE Warming, spicy start, then a massive malt and rye kick with more citrus notes. Very malty middle then the softness stiffens as the rye takes hold. Some attractive corn oiliness makes an arrival for the middle.

FINISH Short to medium with a slight zinginess of rye still holding out but the vanilla from the oak finding its way through.

COMMENTS What a charming little whiskey this is. Not a big bourbon, fragile almost. The rye and malt all but dance on the palate. Perhaps the most complex of the non-small batch Beam brands and being a humble 4-year-old, this is a sensationally outstanding whiskey for its youth. If you've never tasted this, go and grab a bottle now if you can. Superb. And one of my favourites. Certainly the best of its lightweight genre.

OLD GRAND-DAD

It was while downing a very large Old Grand-Dad – my victor's reward after a gargantuan tussle with a plate-sized T-bone steak – that I first genuinely discovered that bourbon played no second fiddle to Scotch. That was in the early '80s while in Washington and though I had been drinking bourbon – when I could get it – for a decade this was the first time I looked upon it with something approaching awe.

For that reason Old Grand-Dad will always have a special place in my heart and to this day I still keep a bottle of the stuff bottled in the late 70s or early 80s in amongst my library of 6,000 whiskies. The whiskey I discovered that evening had been distilled on the eastern fringes of Frankfort on the banks of Elkhorn Creek, close to the Forks of Elkhorn, where the north and south Elkhorn meet. The Elkhorn is an impressive waterway, meandering haphazardly northwards until it eventually crashes into the equally serpentine Kentucky. Sadly, that distillery is no more. Buildings still stand, but silently and the only action seen is not in the old stillhouse but in the massive lorry parks as shipments of Jim Beam come and go. All Old Grand-Dad is now made at Clermont and Boston. There was another Old Grand-Dad distillery, in Louisville, that was abandoned in the 1940s when owners National bought the old distillery on Elkhorn Creek. Like Old Crow and Old Taylor it has been in the hands of Jim Beam since 1987. Originally the distillery was started in the early 1880s by Raymond Heydon, a third-generation distiller in Kentucky. He named the distillery, and brand after his old grand-dad Basil Heydon who had begun the dynasty, and it is he who is depicted on each bottle today.

Of the three Grand-Dad brands, none quite matches up to the extraordinary richness offered by the Frankfort Grand-Dad, though the 100 proof version is a very drinkable whiskey. Hats off to Beam, though, for at least sticking with the original high rye recipe in a bid to try to make the match as close as possible. But again it is fate that has the last word: Old Grand-Dad has kind of come home, because 80 years ago the distillery, in its pre-Louisville days, was located at Hobbs, Bullitt County, which is about two miles from Beam's Clermont Distillery. Spooky.

OLD GRAND-DAD
100 PROOF

NOSE Crisp and fruity. The rye has a big early say, but the sweetness also comprises stewed apples and cinnamon. The most attractive of the Grand-Dad brands, by several miles.

TASTE Very sweet arrival on the palate, surprisingly so. Other Grand-Dads are eye-wateringly dry by contrast at the beginning then sweeten up. This starts sweet and fades to a dryness as an almost chalky vanilla takes a grip.

FINISH Sweetens out and spices up as the rye take hold yet again. A certain vanilla, caramel toffee arrives at the very death, but is well shepherded by the rye.

COMMENTS This is a genuinely attractive whiskey. The rye has a much bigger say than the other Grand-Dad brands and is the better for it. Very clean and crisp throughout and ultimately a highly satisfying glassful with no disappointments.

OLD GRAND-DAD
114 PROOF

A very out of sorts bourbon, this. Harsh and nothing seems to quite hang together. The finish, in particular, needs attention.

OLD GRAND-DAD
(SPECIAL RESERVE)
86 PROOF

Once one of the great whiskies of the world, this is a pale and shallow imitation. It is pleasant enough, but ultimately one is frustrated and disappointed by the lack of depth and direction. Maybe if it didn't have such a great tradition to follow, one might not feel quite so let down by it.

OLD TAYLOR

There is probably no more remarkable sight in all the bourbon industry than the Old Taylor distillery on McCracken Pike near Millville, south of Frankfort. The distillery building, constructed in 1887, is made entirely from local limestone in the turreted form of a castle. The man who built it, the formidable Col. Edmund H. Taylor Jr, certainly knew how to make an impression.

He had already owned Labrot and Graham and the OFC (now Ancient Age) distilleries nearby, and been a founding partner in the Gaines company which built the Old Crow distillery next door. But when he bought the land of the old Johnson distillery he went to town and showed that this was where he would finally lay his hat. He even constructed an ornate springhouse which became a meeting place for local dignitaries.

The distilleries on Glenns Creek enjoyed a great reputation for the quality of their whiskey and Taylor's was no exception. Indeed, Taylor went to extreme lengths to safeguard the quality of his and other genuine bourbon distillers' products. He was the eloquent and energetic driving force behind the Bottled In Bond Act of 1897, which was brought out to protect the public – and the bourbon trade – from an ever-swelling tide of false whiskey. Unscrupulous rectifiers were passing as bourbon spirits that contained most things but. By the time the Act was passed, finding straight bourbon or rye whiskey had become a major achievement indeed. As it happened, the first BIB came from the Old Hermitage distillery on 17 June 1897, just a mile or two up the Kentucky river in south Frankfort. It must have been one of the few distilleries in the Frankfort area he had never had a hand in.

Even so, along with Jim Crow, Taylor became one of the most influential distillers of the 19th century. He died, aged 90, in 1922. Eleven years earlier he had sold out to the American Medicinal Spirits Company of Louisville, who in 1931 also swallowed up Old Crow, before they, too, were swallowed whole by National Distillers in 1936.

Taylor who had at one time been bankrupt, had battled back with the sale of his business to become very wealthy indeed. Doubtless, placing his profits in his local bank would have given him a thrill of satisfaction, having begun his working life as a humble bank cashier in Lexington in 1852.

Today the distillery is owned by a former Old Crow employee Cecil Withrow who bought the entire plant and surrounding grounds from Jim Beam. He has tried to keep the old place in one piece and to help finance that he has set up an antiques mall for visitors to the area.

He is set to launch a 4-year-old 100 proof

Old Stonecastle bourbon in 1998. Although he is sworn to secrecy as to where it was distilled, other than saying it was not Jim Beam or any old stocks of Old Taylor, what I tasted was quite magnificent and very similar to an Ancient Age a year older. He is also hoping to have his own still running by the end of the year: not like the massive stills in the Old Taylor stillhouse, but a smaller one which may have seen some illicit activity in its day.

Old Taylor has changed markedly over recent years. And each time it changes it gets lighter in character. This may well be due to a policy by Jim Beam to use up their existing stocks of old National Distillers products, be it Old Crow, Old Grand-Dad or Old Taylor. Even today in the USA you are likely to find four versions of Old Taylor. The second best is the one that has hung around the shelves longest with the classic Old Taylor label with a portrait of Col. Edmund Haynes Taylor and the Castle Distillery, "Erected in 1887", both in separate boxed compartments on the label. The real giveaway is that it is still at 86 proof, as opposed to 80, and "Aged 6 Years" is marked boldly in red and black lettering. This has a superbly weighted, fruity nose with confident rye and sweet vanilla amid drier tannins. It is sweet on the palate, too, again with impressive weight with first rich corn and oak and then a delightful rye follow-through.

A degree lighter is its successor, an 80-proof

version with only a red border around the "Aged 6 Years". The incredible, more harmonic, nose harnesses less oak weight and the corn now tends towards something a little younger, fresher and sweeter with a hint of green, unripe apple that perhaps has something to do with succulent, mouthwatering rye. It is friskier on the palate, also, with a bigger corn dominance towards the middle. The finish, though, reveals some definite rye riches and aged oak to guarantee solidity.

OLD TAYLOR • 6-YEAR-OLD • 80 PROOF

NOSE Big sweet corn and light vanilla. The rye and almost smoky oakiness associated with phases I and II have now entirely vanished.

TASTE Fresh and refreshing; gentle peppers help bring extra life to the laid-back vanilla and sweet, demerara sugar.

FINISH Slightly disappointing. There is an eggy, French toast sweetness and a small hint of small grain complexity. The oak never rises above soft vanilla.

COMMENTS Overall, an enjoyable whiskey, but not particularly rich or challenging for a 6-year-old. The older "National"-based versions have that wonderful, distinctive rye character and win hands down. It appears that Beam have tried to make the change from old stock to new by blending in Beam with the old in ever-increasing amounts to make the transition a smooth one for drinkers; an understandable stance to take. However, I always thought they would have been better off bringing out the old stuff as special bottlings instead. A noble try, none the less.

This is excellent stuff.

The third age of Old Taylor sees a switch in label to a more streamlined version and is instantly recognizable in that the label actually spells the distillery's founder incorrectly – "Hayes" rather than Haynes.

The current version has the Haynes name restored, but the whiskey is a shade lighter still and has "Jim Beam" written all over its fresh, fruity character.

BERNHEIM

At some time during 1996 a bottle of Stitzel Weller 4-year-old became Stitzel Weller by name only. In fact the first Bernheim straight whiskey had been bottled. It was a situation peculiar to the American whiskey industry and one of those things that makes explaining the genesis of the nation's bourbons and rye a very hard task indeed.

In other words to taste Bernheim you must taste Stitzel Weller, although if in Louisville you might have thought there was a Stitzel Weller distillery already. There is, but it closed in 1992. So when the latest bottlings of standard Old Fitz were filled, it came from the brand spanking new distillery, Bernheim, opened the same year, initially to replace the dilapidated Belmont and Astore Distilleries which had formerly occupied the site. Sad to say, the new 4-year-old Old Fitz is no better than the last one. That was always Old Fitz's Achilles heel and apart from some extra pepperiness there is no improvement to the flatness of the old whiskey. But that doesn't mean to say that the whiskey of Bernheim is doomed to failure. It just seems that that particular style of wheated bourbon takes a long time to get going and this is proved by some of the sublime

Left
I W Bernheim c. 1900. Despite only recently becoming the name of a bourbon conglomerate, the Bernheim family and whiskey go way back.

Stitzel moments you can experience.

The Bernheim distillery inside and out is a testimony to 1990s' efficiency. Their entire plant is made from stainless steel, except for the heads of the two beer stills, which are both made from copper. One still has been designated to make the brands

Above
Originally a
whiskey
merchant,
Bernheim
eventually built
his own distillery
by the railroad
tracks in
Louisville at the
turn of the
century.

for which Bernheim was originally constructed, i.e. IW Harper and Old Charter rye-recipe ranges and the other for the Stitzel Weller brands, namely Weller, Old Fitzgerald and Rebel Yell.

At least the surrounding warehouses, massive all-brick constructions so typical of Louisville, still stand and form an astonishing backdrop to the distillery. Although the Bernheim name is new as far as being a distillery is concerned, it is, in fact, one of the most famous names in bourbon history. Isaac "Ike" Bernheim originated from Pennsylvania and with his brother Bernard began a whiskey business, initially buying their product from others. But at

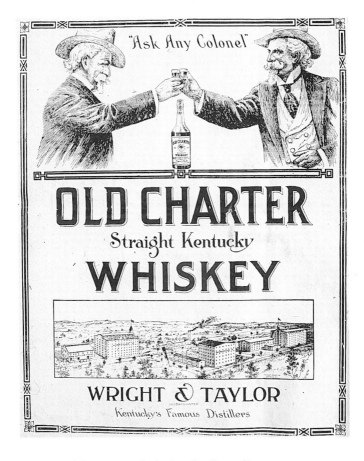

the turn of the century Ike built a distillery of his own. The brand which made their fortune was IW Harper, a name chosen because they considered Bernheim a particularly un-distilling sounding moniker. Actually, the IW initials were

Above
An Old Charter magazine ad. from 1913.

113

Ike's but the Harper was a horse-owning friend amongst whose property was the very Tavern in which Jesse James' mother was born.

At the moment all the IW Harper and Old Charter whiskey found around the world is the fruit of the old Belmont distillery. Except possibly for the IW Harper Gold Medal which will very shortly be switching to Bernheim whiskey. It will be the first rye recipe whiskey on the market from the distillery.

There has of late been a whiskey from the Astore distillery which was demolished with Belmont. That was found in Henry Clay, a one-off brand that has come and gone. If you see one anywhere grab it. Or better still let me know and I'll grab it! This is a 1980 distillation bottled as 16-year-old and a cracker rich in honeycomb and spice complexity.

However, as I write this in early 1998 there are doubts about the Bernheim distillery. It will not be closed, but with Bernheim's owners, United Distillers, merging with IDV to form Diageo, all these brands might be considered to be of secondary importance within the new company structure. Max Shapira of Heaven Hill has been eyeing the plant as a replacement for his destroyed Heaven Hill complex. At the time of writing he hasn't made up his mind, but if I were a betting man my money would be on Bernheim becoming the next Heaven Hill distillery.

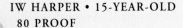
**IW HARPER • 15-YEAR-OLD
80 PROOF**

NOSE A graceful, sturdy nose. The hint of mint present in the 12-year-old has come through much louder here. The oak is also noticeable with a pine-fresh menthol effect. When really warm there is even some sweaty saddle leather. Really! Delightful.

TASTE Surprisingly sweet start. Very vague traces of maple sugar cling to the palate as the grain, especially the corn registers loud and clear.

FINISH The finish starts as sweet as when the whiskey first hit the palate. Its decay to dryness takes an age and in that time there is a very impressive show of toffee and fruit, possibly fresh dates.

COMMENTS If you could combine the nose of the 12-year-old with the taste of the 15, you would have a very formidable whiskey. Nevertheless, this is a superstar whiskey with sacksful of character. Always seems to be slightly different every time I taste it, but never fails to fall into the sweet charmer category. Beautiful and not to be wasted with either ice or water. Take it as it comes to bring out its full complexity.

IW HARPER GOLD MEDAL • 80 PROOF

NOSE Firm, grainy and well spiced. Sweet vanilla hangs in there, too. And maybe a hint of butter for good measure.

TASTE Young, bitter grains let rip on first arrival in mouth. As the taste develops, the corn becomes quite powerful. Never sits still and spices up towards the middle.

FINISH Lots of corn oil and dry oak towards the end. Very big flavour development even at the last.

COMMENTS "Smooth and soft" on the palate as described by the Bernheim boys. I'm not so sure, though. There is lots of youth displayed in this whiskey and I love the way it really takes off in the mouth. Smooth and soft usually describes pretty docile whiskies: this one is anything but.

IW HARPER 101 • 101 PROOF

Not the most complex whiskey you'll ever find, but a really enjoyable high proof journey over concentrated corn!

IW HARPER PRESIDENT'S RESERVE

NOSE The star of the Harper show. Prickly peppers just tease as you try to concentrate on the orangey toffee main theme. A hint of toffee mint can be found, as well, plus a strata of malt. Excellent balance between sweet and dry throughout.

TASTE Delicate, though nothing like as complex as the nose. Medium sweet as the Harper toffee character rumbles through gradually deepening in character as the oak presence builds up.

FINISH Quite dry with hickory and a certain smokiness.

COMMENTS A genuinely pleasant whiskey. The nose is sensational, perhaps too good. I do love that Harper toffee character and here it acts as a decent brake to keep that build-up of oak in check.

IW HARPER
12-YEAR-OLD
86 PROOF

Beautiful aroma of diced orange peel, green melon, raisins and fresh custard all topped with an assortment of spices makes for a satisfying bourbon.

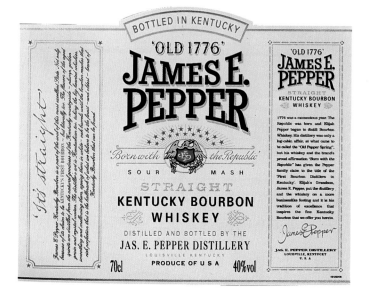

JAMES E. PEPPER • 80 PROOF

NOSE Pepper by name, pepper by nature. Very warm and spicy.

TASTE Quite young character displayed by a tell-tale fizziness. Links quite well with a soft charred bitterness which sits well with the sweeter corn.

FINISH Quite short with mounting vanilla toffee.

COMMENTS Some bottlings can be a lot gentler and sweeter than this, especially on the nose and early palate. At its best it can be really impressive; the average bottle is less enthralling but succeeds in being a pretty tasty and moreish beverage none the less.

OLD CHARTER
8-YEAR-OLD
80 PROOF

NOSE Those who reckon all bourbons are much the same should get a nose of this. Classic stuff, not in that honeyed way that perhaps the very greatest bourbon attract you, but in its hot pepper and cloves aroma which actually masks the honey lurking somewhere underneath. A nose to get the adrenalin running. When it has oxidised in the glass for 10 minutes or so the honey begins to assume command as the peppers recede.

TASTE Excellent start on the palate, with intriguing sweet and sour with spice. The middle is something else again with the rye making a very pleasant and full contribution.

FINISH Long and ultimately disappointing. The dryness which evolves does not take a particular shape. It just seems to keep any developing sweetness at bay. The result is slightly metallic and a little sappy.

COMMENTS This is a whiskey not so much of two halves but a quarter and three quarters.

OLD CHARTER
10-YEAR-OLD
86 PROOF

Big, confident start with enormous dry oak presence and house-style spice. Then it sweetens with the heavy bouquet one might sometimes find by night in a heavily stocked summer garden. The finish falls away a little.

OLD CHARTER CLASSIC
12-YEAR-OLD • 90 PROOF

NOSE Very fresh, lavender and cream toffee.

TASTE Surprisingly crisp and small grain dominant. The rye and malt really do come through with a clattering vigour. Lots of big oak arrives for the middle, but does not outstay its welcome.

FINISH Big finale with lots of ground cocoa and a resweetening through toffee.

COMMENTS This is delicious. A real hard nut, full of rigid grain and exquisite dark chocolate. I really do love this style of bourbon, one you must spend time to get to know.

OLD CHARTER PROPRIETOR'S RESERVE
13-YEAR-OLD • 90 PROOF

NOSE Wonderfully subtle; lots of acacia honey and butter caramel toffee mingle beautifully with ripe, sweet plums. Glorious.

TASTE A real flavour explosion to start, but a controlled one. A hint of cinnamon sparks off a spicy initial mouth-feel, then there is rapid free-falling into dry, toasty notes as the vanillins from oak take hold.

FINISH Long, lingering, liquorice and toast.

COMMENTS Superb stuff, genuinely complex and a rare example of where age has highlighted rather than dimmed the very finest notes a distillery is able to produce. Very subtle and understated in its parts; the whole, however, paints a very large and impressive picture on the palate.

EARLY TIMES

Opposite
The Brown-
Forman offices
in Louisville,
once a proud
distillery, still
retain the
landmark Old
Forester bottle-
shaped water
tower.

A short distance east of Bardstown, sandwiched between the Blue Grass Parkway and route 62 is a small town called Early Times. It sounds like a place where whiskey making should be in full swing, though you will find no working distillery there. As is the manner of these things, quite peculiar to Kentucky, it has upped and gone, leaving only a community christened in its memory.

Instead, you will find the distillery some distance away at Shively on the outskirts of Louisville. Unlike its long abandoned namesake, it was not built as the Early Times distillery, though. It began life in 1935 as the Old Kentucky Distillery and became part of the Brown-Forman portfolio just five years later when they acquired it at roughly the same time as the much prettier Labrot and Graham plant, though for a lot more money. Later it became the Early Times distillery.

There is nothing simple or straightforward in the journeys Kentucky distilleries have taken to reach their present state, meandering through history like the great river itself. And Early Times is about as complicated as it gets, demonstrating how brands move around Kentucky in a manner which can leave the head spinning.

The old distillery at Early Times was originally

part of the extended Beam empire. It was founded by John M. Beam, better known as Jack. He was grandson of the Jacob Beam who first began distilling in 1788 and Jack's first enterprise, founded in 1860, soon located on a site on Stuart's Creek, about six miles east of Bardstown, that came to be known as Beam's station. His first brand was called, unromantically, "AG Hall", perhaps something to do with his new bride's maiden name. Aged just 21 when he set up his distillery, Jack was showing great confidence in his whiskey and this was rewarded when in 1886 he formed with two others the Early Times Distillery Company with a capital of $45,000, each share being worth $100. Five years later a new, much larger distillery was built a mile or two closer to Bardstown. A railroad station was built beside the distillery, so the area became known as Early Times Station, then as a community grew up around it, simply Early Times. By 1909 there were four brands being marketed by the company. Three of them, AG Hall, Brookhill and JT Beam were all straight four-year-old bourbons. Only one was an eight-year-old and that was Early Times. It appeared that people, even then, were prepared to pay a few extra cents for finer quality.

By the time of Jack's death in 1913 Early Times was sold not only locally but as far afield as California, Texas and Arkansas. It was only in 1916 that it began to pick up markets in the east. But it was all to no avail. Prohibition saw the closure of the distillery and in 1923 the then owner, S.L. Guthrie, who had started work there 16 years earlier as an office boy, sold the company to Brown-Forman who were hunting stocks of whiskey as they were one of the few companies who had been granted a licence to sell it for medicinal purposes. The distillery was finally abandoned a year later when the government, through the Concentration Warehouse Act, refused Brown-Forman permission to continue keeping the whiskey at Early Times, Nelson County. All stocks were then moved to Louisville.

That was not all the whiskey Brown-Forman moved at that time. They were likewise forced to close and dismantle their St Mary distillery south of Lorreto, Marion County, where their famed Old Forester whisky was produced. For the first time and certainly not the last, the whiskies of Early Times and Old Forester were to be very closely linked.

At Early Times today an unusual situation has arisen: another whiskey is made there which is very much, almost infinitely, better than the brand from which the distillery takes its name. Really, it could only happen in Kentucky, and once more it is down to the extraordinary way in which distilleries open and close around the state with production being transferred here and there. It is all very confusing. But one fact is very simple: Old Forester is a far better whiskey than Early Times.

Above
The Old Forester
site in Louisville
when it was still
a working
distillery.

In 1979 Brown-Forman closed the Old Forester distillery in Louisville and moved production to their Early Times plant. But though the same stills were used to make the whiskeys, those whiskeys were very different indeed. Old Forester enjoys a much higher rye content than Early Times and this accounts for greater depth, complexity and finish. Indeed, in America Early Times can no longer be found as a straight bourbon at all. The whiskey is matured in used oak barrels. The only Early Times bourbon found today is sold in Japan. And it is a long way from being the eight-years age statement old Jack Beam used to cherish.

Other whiskey made there is corn and rye which is used as a flavouring factor in the blending of Canadian Mist whiskey. But during 1997 another entirely different whiskey was made at the plant: Heaven Hill's. After the catastrophic fire which consumed that distillery in November 1996, production was transferred on contract basis to Early Times. In so doing, the history of Early Times distillery turned a strange full circle, because keeping a close eye on the production of their own special recipe whiskey was distiller Parker Beam and his son Craig. As it happens, Parker Beam is grandnephew of the great Jim Beam. Who, in turn, happened to be the nephew of Jack Beam, founder of Early Times...

EARLY TIMES PREMIUM • 74.2 PROOF

A straight bourbon available only in Japan and made to a 79 per cent corn, 11 per cent rye, 10 per cent malted barley formula. The whiskey used is around 5.5 years old.

NOSE Soft and simple. Some chalky vanilla slightly sweetened by a big corn presence.

TASTE A slightly raw, harsh and imbalanced start. Corn oil sits attractively on roof of mouth to quieten things down but some wild oakiness battles through.

FINISH Just a little caramel, but not enough. Slightly bitter and rough.

COMMENTS It's OK for bourbons to be rough and ready, which this is, but I like to see either the small grains win through to give complexity or a sweetish nature emerging from somewhere. Neither happens.

OLD FORESTER

This is another whiskey to have at one stage turned full circle. Oddly enough, it began life because George Gavin Brown, a Kentuckian of proud Scottish descent, took to heart a sad observation by a physician friend that the bourbon he needed to administer to the sick was often of dubious quality. Brown made a point of buying high-grade bourbon from different distillers, mixing it together and selling it partly for medicinal purposes. For good measure he sealed all his bottles, making the Old Forester brand the first to be sold in this quality-assuring manner.

That was some time in the 1870s, but 60 years on the company could have folded like so many others because of Prohibition. But the Browns decided to fight to the bitter end and they were successful in their bid to gain a licence to sell bourbon during that bleak period – again for medicinal purposes only. Old Forester which started off as an aid to the ill was back on prescription again.

The forefathers of George Gavin Brown had been amongst the first to conquer and settle the wildlands of Kentucky. Even so, he made no play on his family's achievements and instead there is today still debate over just why he called his prized whiskey Old Forester. A clue is that it was originally spelt with two "r"s, as opposed to the single one today. That would neatly tie in with Dr William Forester, a leading physician of his day whom he might easily have supplied. Others once claimed it was in honour of the Confederate General, Nathan Bedford Forrest. Or simply it was a mis-spelt attempt to honour lumberjacks of the Mississippi and Ohio valleys. Take your pick.

Although the spelling has changed, there is one part of the label which has withstood the test of time: George Brown's carefully written note on the front: "This whisky is distilled by us only and we are responsible for its richness and fine quality. Its elegant flavor is solely due to original fineness developed with care. There is nothing better in the market."

For years the old distillery in Louisville could be picked out for miles around on account of a water tower shaped like a bottle of Old Forester.

However, the distillery closed in 1979 and all production was moved over to Brown-Forman's Early Times plant. The bottle remains a landmark, but only for the corporation's head office.

OLD FORESTER • 86 PROOF
The standard bottling aged around 58 months and distilled from the classic 72/18/10 mashbill.

NOSE Beautifully floral. Violets and honeysuckle are both present with a hint of hickory smoke and some lovely rye fruitiness. Excellent.

TASTE Drier to start than the nose suggests although the rye makes an early impact. The second wave of flavours to hit the taste-buds is sweeter with toffee and oranges, but this is very short lived. The rye returns with some corn and butter.

FINISH Medium length and very dry. Some spices pep up the finish. Oak has the final say.

COMMENTS This is a beautifully constructed whisky. At no one moment does it sit still on the palate, changing shape and character second by second. Fine stuff.

OLD FORESTER • BIB • 100 PROOF

One by-product of Prohibition was the birth of this excellent bourbon. One of the laws surrounding the sale of bourbon during Prohibition was that it had to be bottled in bond. That meant it was minimum 4 years of age and 100 proof. This one is a 5-year-old.

NOSE Much the same as the 86 proof except heavier honey and spice. Also a little bit waxy.

TASTE Big, lurching start again with big rye follow-through. Little if any citrus around on this one. Less complex although the peppers are quite warming.

FINISH More rye towards the end and some butter. Liquorice and toffee vie for the final spot. Some very dry oak hangs about, too.

COMMENTS Another real mouthful of a whisky. Enormous character and the rye is prevalent throughout. Perhaps not quite so subtle and satisfying as the 86 proof, though.

FORESTER BARREL RESERVE 96 • 96 PROOF

A special edition brought out to commemorate the 1996 Olympics held in Atlanta, Georgia. Beautifully weighted, creamy and brittle with lingering rye. Gold-medal stuff with great stamina and poise. Superb.

FORESTER 1870 • 80 PROOF

Younger brother to the Old Forester, aged at around 49 months. In the last year or two 1870 has made a welcome addition to the undersubscribed array of bourbons available in the UK.

NOSE Lively and playful like a young pup. It appears to be similar in age to the Early Times Yellow Label, but it is remarkable what just a few extra small grains can do. The rye is discernible here and gives an oily weight.

TASTE The rye is the first to show, crashing awkwardly against the taste-buds, but certainly making itself noticed. The corn arrives on the third and fourth waves and blends in attractively. Neat and tidy complexity.

FINISH Here it disappoints a little showing lack of maturity. Austere and oaky with a little oil perhaps from the rye just hanging on to give extra length.

COMMENTS This is not a classic whisky, but it is highly enjoyable. Because of the youth and lightness of the bourbon, the rye is able to have quite a profound say. Very tasty indeed.

Two other whiskies to be made from the Old Forester recipe at Early Times are Woodford Reserve and President's Reserve (see Labrot and Graham).

Above

*A ancient specimen of Old Forester made before Prohibition
but not bottled until 1930.*

FOUR ROSES

If legend is to be believed, then the remains that can be found a mile or two past the railroad crossing on Bond's Mill Road to the south of Lawrenceburg are one of Kentucky's oldest distilleries: the ancient Old Joe distillery. But these remains pall in comparison to the extraordinary lemon-yellow vista of its neighbouring present-day rival: the Four Roses distillery (still better known to most locals as Old Prentice).

Four Roses is something of an enigma in the USA. Everybody has heard of it, but few I have met actually realise that such a distillery exists – even those behind the counter in liquor stores. In America, until the last year or so it could be found only as a blend, a mixture of straight bourbon and neutral grain spirits. Even in the 1960s adverts celebrated the soufflé-light nature of this whiskey by depicting a glass of the stuff anchored to the ground while a bottle of it floated off. The strange twist is, American drinkers are slowly discovering that its straight bourbon possesses similar characteristics.

It was not always the case. Until 1986 Four Roses was made at a massive all-brick affair at Shively, Louisville, just around the corner from Early Times. The six-year-old which entered

Europe from there was a whiskey of proportions as immense and chunky as the distillery itself. It was a fat whiskey with lots of chocolate and cocoa tones and a finish as long and complex as the brand's history. It was a much ballsier whiskey when the American public were at last able to get their hands on it.

Instead, the present distillery can take a certain pride in producing probably the most delicate of Kentucky's bourbons. Being owned by Seagram there is enormous emphasis on quality and, typical of their North American operation, they go to extraordinary lengths to create and continue a selected style.

They achieve this by making in the region of eleven different types of whiskey, with variances on the mashbill, the types of yeast used and so on. Maturation has also been carefully thought about. On the other side of the road from Four Roses are a cluster of ironclads, but none of them houses Seagram distillate. Instead it is the rich aroma of Wild Turkey which catches on the breeze. You will find future Four Roses on a large site on the road to Jim Beam and Bardstown at Cox Creek. There warehouses are many and low slung, the theory being that the barrels will each receive identical heating.

The Four Roses has a long pedigree. In 1888 a man called Paul Jones brought it to Kentucky from his home state Georgia. Whether he took the name from his fiancee, who was said to have

Above
The Four Roses
distillery –
known to the
locals as "Old
Prentice".

worn four roses as a symbol of their betrothal, or from four young ladies he knew by the name of Rose, no one knows. But it certainly stuck. Now there will be another name to contend with. Seagram have just purchased a brand called Bulleit for home and Japanese consumption, and one which previously contained four-year-old Ancient Age.

Before entering the distillery to have a look around, you cannot help but stand outside for a while and stare at the building with something approaching incredulity. I have been to over 150 whiskey distilleries spanning four continents, but every time I drop in to Four Roses I just have to feast my eyes upon its classic Spanish facade: there is nothing like it anywhere in the world. It dates back to 1910 and no one knows for sure why it was designed in such a style, even complete with bell tower. But thankfully though Seagram have owned it since 1940. During this time the famous old McKenna distillery in Fairfield has gone, along with plants at Athertonville, Midway, Cynthiana, and two in Louisville, but this distillery has not only survived, it has been left in all its old glory.

Indeed, even inside the building something truly remarkable is happening. Each time I have wandered round, the old cypress fermenters have looked just a little more jaded, nearing the end of a very old and worthwhile life. Some have already been replaced by metal ones and I fear it is only a matter of time before the remaining wood will be ripped away.

That has, in fact, started to happen already. But instead of being replaced by soul-less metal fermenters, new – or should I say old – cypress ones are taking their place. Cypress is becoming near enough impossible to find in America today. But manager Jim Rutledge heard of a scheme by which old cypress logs were being dragged up from river bottoms where they had lain for some 150 years. Jim has to order the wood for the new fermenters a year in advance as it takes that long to successfully dry the cypress without any ill effects. The first brand new-old fermenters are now in place.

It is fitting to note that these trees were still growing in 1818 when old Joe Peyton paddled his way down the Kentucky until he found a pleasant clearing with a spring near by to set up home and almost immediately a distillery. Just a few hundred yards behind the Four Roses distillery the remnants of the stone distillery which replaced the wooden one still stand. "You'll find nothing in there except maybe an angry copperhead or two," former manager Ova Haney warned me when I first told him I was going to have a look around. Already I had seen first hand the wily reluctance of legendary Wild Turkey distiller Jimmy Russell to head too far into the bush to show me what still stood of the old Tyrone distilleries, in case he happened upon something very unpleasant. For that reason I have never fully inspected Old Joe's place, a case of the spineless in fear of the legless.

FOUR ROSES
80 PROOF

NOSE Extremely light and slightly floral with a zesty lemon and/or orange peel. Just a little spirity but the delicate complexity makes amends. Just a little rye hangs around, too.

TASTE Thin start on the mouth and disappointingly bitter at first. But this rather negative beginning soon vanishes and is replaced by a lovely vanilla and malt which is altogether more satisfying.

FINISH The delicacy continues. The oak is present in soft vanilla caramel tones and there is a return of bitterness, but like powdered cocoa.

COMMENTS A quite beautiful nose is well matched by a soft, almost complex character which arrives after a sluggish start. One of Kentucky's lighter bourbons yet an enjoyable one, all the same.

FOUR ROSES BLACK LABEL 86 PROOF

NOSE Distinctly malty with confident vanilla. Less fruit than the younger version and much heavier without becoming at all oak dominant.

TASTE Sweet vanilla start followed by a wave of powerful rye. The small grains play a significant role and make for a tasty, lip-smacking and spicy bourbon.

FINISH Shades of dark pepper and treacle. Sounds awful but in fact the weight is brilliant. The vanilla comes on very strong on the finish as the oak grabs hold.

COMMENTS Really lovely stuff, this. The oak plays a starring role here, but the malt and rye guarantee balance. Very good indeed.

FOUR ROSES SINGLE BARREL RESERVE
86 PROOF

The nose is so in tune it sings lullabies. But after that it flattens a little on the palate and is saved by an excellent rye backbone. A hit or miss affair but congratulations to Four Roses for producing the corked stopper with the biggest pop when first opened!

FOUR ROSES • SUPER PREMIUM
86 PROOF

NOSE Very spicy, rye-rich nose. There is also an intriguing mixture of new leather, stewed apples and corn.

TASTE Rich, sweet, oily mouth-feel. Excellent weight and poise throughout as the chewable cream toffee takes command.

FINISH Lots of caramel on the finish, some dried dates and spicy fruit cake in there, too. Finally the oak wins through with lots of vanilla.

COMMENTS Well structured and beautifully balanced. It is unique among the Four Roses brands for its fatness on the palate. Absolutely delicious.

HEAVEN HILL

Opposite
The Heaven Hill distillery as it will be fondly remembered, shortly before it was destroyed by fire in 1996.

It is the forces of nature that give so much to bourbon. The sun beats down on North American soil to help grow the corn, rye, wheat and barley that go into her whiskies; rain pours, sometimes incessantly, to intermingle with her ancient limestone and it is the sun again which helps the spirit breathe into the oak that grows so abundantly with her help. But nature also takes away. And so it was that in November 1996 that the Heaven Hill distillery was consumed by an awesome conflagration, the flames fanned by pitiless winds.

When daylight came on 7 November, there was still smoke rising from dampened ashes. Some warehouses had all but vanished in the inferno, an entire road had melted under the heat of a river of blazing alcohol and the distillery building was a shell, its distilling apparatus buckled and useless.

It was not the first distillery to have so perished. During the 19th century, especially in

the time of copper pots, it was almost a regular
occurrence. But this was different. Kentucky was
already down to eleven working distilleries, that
number increased only a year or so before with
the advent of Labrot and Graham. The loss of
nine warehouses represented a significant gouge
into bourbon stocks. Companies over the years

had been under- rather than overproducing. So it was imperative that Heaven Hill whiskey be made again as soon as possible.

Although one of Kentucky's last two working family-owned distilleries had been lost, the spirit that had brought it into being was still very much in evidence. Vice President Max Shapira had to quickly get over the shock of losing his distillery situated close by his offices on the outskirts of Bardstown. He immediately looked into rebuilding but first tried to buy in as much lost stock as possible from elsewhere and struck a deal with the other family distillers, Brown-Forman, in hiring their Early Times distillery for four days a week to make bourbon.

And making bourbon is what Heaven Hill are all about. They are the proprietors of more name brands than a book this size could list. The number runs into hundreds, some of them tiny case sales in obscure markets. If any customer, either in the US or abroad, needed bourbon it was at Heaven Hill they would enquire first. And, usually, it was from there they would end up getting their supplies. When you buy an own label supermarket or otherwise obscure brand, chances are the bottle will tell you that it's Bardstown whiskey. And the 99.9 per cent chance is that Heaven Hill will be responsible.

This had been the case since 1935 when the Shapira brothers built the distillery beside a small creek on the Loretto road heading south out of

Opposite
Barrels are
moved around
the warehouse in
order to benefit
from a change of
temperature –
from the lower
(cooler) parts to
the higher
(warmer) reaches
of the warehouse.

town. But it is only in the last two decades since Max has been in control that the distillery has been better known for some astonishingly high-quality own brands. It was Max who set up a policy of branding, choosing to concentrate on the name of early bourbon pioneers such as Elijah Craig and Evan Williams.

Heaven Hill whiskey does not really shine until it passes the six-year mark. Then it positively blossoms. And one of the great tragedies is that a distillery has been lost which made some of the finest bourbon to be found in all Kentucky. When tasting in Japan once, I came across the Evan Williams twelve-year-old and was stunned to uncustomary silence by its

extraordinary depth. But you don't have to wait that long for Heaven Hill whiskey: at half that age it is a bourbon to take very seriously.

One of the charms of Heaven Hill is the fact that it made corn as well as some exceptional rye whiskey. Again, the markets were small but the company went to the trouble to keep tradition alive. It is unlikely that it shall be doing so from the burnt-out remains of the old distillery. At first Max had plans to build again. But there are winds of fluctuating fortune in business too and a year is a long time in the whiskey world. Since that fire United Distillers, owners of Stitzel Weller and Bernheim, have merged with IDV to form a super-company. The talk in Kentucky is

Below
The latest graduates from the bottling line.

that the new company Diageo might be happy to off-load some of their bourbon concern, which is a relatively minor player in the market, in order to concentrate on their Scotch brands and possibly Dickel. That being so, Bernheim is surplus to requirements and Max has closely scrutinized the distillery both from within and on the balance sheet. At the time of writing he has not made up his mind. But when this book goes into a second edition don't be surprised if Heaven Hill whiskey is being made in Louisville.

HEAVEN HILL • 80 PROOF

Called Old Style or White Label. This is the standard HH brand. In Ohio, Georgia and Tennessee and various other places it is found as a green label. Young, hard and uncompromising: proof positive that Heaven Hill really does need a few extra years on the standard 4 to get all cylinders firing. Bland and rather untamed.

HEAVEN HILL • 6-YEAR-OLD • 90 PROOF

NOSE Smoky, mildly phenolic and showing fine maturity. The nose suggests that this is a bourbon of dignity with excellent weight and just the right amount of sweetness. Hints of violets and rye. Wonderful.

TASTE Bigger than the nose suggests with impressive demerara sugar sweetness linking well with rye and vanilla. A slight and surprising echo of superior pot still rum here.

DISTILLED AND BOTTLED IN
KENTUCKY

HEAVEN HILL.

Symbol of Excellence

KENTUCKY STRAIGHT
BOURBON WHISKEY
45% ALC/VOL (90 PROOF)
DISTILLED AND BOTTLED BY
Heaven Hill Distilleries, Inc.
BARDSTOWN, NELSON COUNTY, KENTUCKY 40004

FINISH Remains sweet on the finish with the oak having a bigger say. A touch of liquorice; still the dark sugar note continues, though very mildly, and allspice to finish.

COMMENTS A very complex whiskey which seems to celebrate that Heaven Hill has passed the 6-year mark and has come to a form of maturity. The character is rather bitty and the different flavours do not mingle easily, but they make for a fascinating and very enjoyable whiskey.

HEAVEN HILL BIB 100 PROOF

The nose is angular, harsh and thin with little balance. This corn-dominated whiskey underlines the fact that Heaven Hill does not really get going until it reaches six years at least. And being BIB it is underlined in bold.

HEAVEN HILL ULTRA DELUXE • 80 PROOF

NOSE Sweet pipe smoke, apples and malted barley make for a light but enjoyable aroma.

TASTE An incredibly sweet kick-off and then very distinctive corn. Clean, sweet and spicy.

FINISH Light with a build-up of chalky vanilla. The dryness is in stark contrast to the very sweet start.

COMMENTS Little complexity here and while the taste does not go anywhere near bearing out the claim on the neck of the bottle that there is "No finer Bourbon in this World", this is a very simple but enjoyable shot.

OLD HEAVEN HILL BIB
100 PROOF

An unsophisticated, mildly enjoyable bourbon, though clearly flawed.

DOWLING DE LUXE BIB

NOSE The most subtly and wonderfully scented of Heaven Hill's BIB range; stunningly sweet but never cloying, lots of oak, apples and grapes. A slight oiliness hangs on, too, and just the faintest hint of spice - even cinnamon. Complex and charming.

TASTE Creamy textured and chewy start and a definite build-up of malt and rye. The small grains - especially the rye - offer juicy fruit which yields to corn.

FINISH Highly complex and spicy. Vanilla from the oak blends beautifully with the lingering rye and grassy barley. A touch of toffee, too.

COMMENTS A really good BIB offering riches you might not expect to find in an HH BIB. Excellent.

ECHO SPRINGS • 80 PROOF

This is a beginner's bourbon; something to wean people away from vodka. Charmingly balanced.

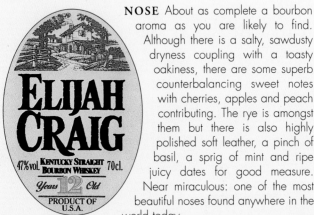

ELIJAH CRAIG • 12-YEAR-OLD • 94 PROOF

For this whiskey there is a maximum of 100 barrels mingled, as against 5-10 times that number for a standard Evan Williams. The choice of barrel has significantly improved over the years so today it is unquestionably one of the great bourbons.

NOSE About as complete a bourbon aroma as you are likely to find. Although there is a salty, sawdusty dryness coupling with a toasty oakiness, there are some superb counterbalancing sweet notes with cherries, apples and peach contributing. The rye is amongst them but there is also highly polished soft leather, a pinch of basil, a sprig of mint and ripe juicy dates for good measure. Near miraculous: one of the most beautiful noses found anywhere in the world today.

TASTE A bourbon to keep in the mouth for ever. Surprisingly dry in comparison with the nose, and the fruit has been lost somewhere en route. But the big oily oaky notes make amends as rye arrives to enrich the middle even further.

FINISH Toffee apples and malt rise above the gentle oaky notes and there is a very late arrival of burnt sugar and rye. The very final notes are extremely complex and hard to define. But there is a bitter, toasty residue that rounds everything off to near perfection.

COMMENTS Perhaps one of my favourite five or six bourbons and certainly the superstar in the Heaven Hill portfolio. It is a bourbon of almost unfathomable depth and has something for everyone. However, there is so much that it's not a bourbon to treat lightly. This is something you build up to. And perhaps at its best just before bed. Brilliant.

ELIJAH CRAIG SINGLE BARREL • 18-YEAR-OLD 90 PROOF

Big and resounding with now more honey than oak. Very fat and sweet and hangs beautifully on the palate.

EVAN WILLIAMS • 7-YEAR-OLD • 90 PROOF

NOSE Slightly sharp and green with a touch of menthol.

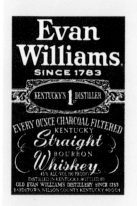

TASTE A very sweet start with soft brown sugars and caramel. As the middle is reached there is a hint of spice and maltiness.

FINISH A gentle finale to a light, easy-going whiskey. Limited vanilla and a little oak sap add extra weight but the small grains, especially the malt, do hang on to the finish.

COMMENTS An easy number, this. A fresh, light weight throughout makes this one not for those looking for the intensity you might expect at 7 years but a gentle, sweet, untaxing journey with not a bump along the way. (NB In California this is found with an identical label but it is 5-year-old and 86 proof.) Not only lighter in colour, it is lighter in nose and body, too, with none of the menthol but a particularly malty theme develops without the spice. Young, malty and refreshing throughout, it is much sweeter on the finish and the corn develops pleasantly. It has made an enormous jump from a HH 4-year-old. Both are mildly impressive in their own way.

EVAN WILLIAMS
8-YEAR-OLD
86 PROOF

Not found in the USA, this is a European and Pacific Rim brand. A massive leap from the 7-year-old; the first honied thread can be seen with oily rye, sweetcorn and cocoa on the finish. Not overly complex, but a fine whiskey.

EVAN WILLIAMS • 12-YEAR-OLD • 101 PROOF

For Japan only. This is a 101 version of the Elijah Craig. Some I have tasted has been nearly every bit as good. Others can be heavier and nothing like so subtle on the nose yet its honied intensity really does make you realize just what a fabulous genre bourbon can be. On first tasting this in Japan I was shaken to the core. It was the best "discovery" of the year. Having studied it closely, it wasn't a knee-jerk reaction: this is sublime.

EVAN WILLIAMS • 23-YEAR-OLD • 107 PROOF

For Japan only, only 200 cases a year. The oldest branded bourbon on the market.

NOSE The oak plays major league here yet is not off-key. There is big spice and trademark Heaven Hill honey. Deep and mysterious.

TASTE Amazingly sweet and rich for its age. Still the corn is intact and very fine but the malt comes through with liquid honey. The oak is quite warming for the middle.

FINISH Medium length, solid oak and liquorice but the toffee remains sweet.

COMMENTS This is the grand old man of Kentucky. An astonishing whiskey that defies nature by holding so much stature despite all those blazing 100 degree Kentucky summers. It has no right to be this good: a real marvel.

EVAN WILLIAMS 1783
10-YEAR-OLD
86 PROOF

A curious whiskey, this. It never quite takes off as you might expect; remains very low-key but has enough small grain notes to make for something very enjoyable. It is Master Distiller Parker Beam's favourite HH; mine is two years older.

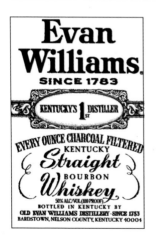

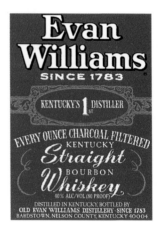

Above

Labels for the 80 and 100 proof variants of the Evan Williams brand.

HENRY MCKENNA SINGLE BARREL BIB 10-YEAR-OLD

(Barrel 32, barreled on 12/14/84.)

NOSE
There is a peppery pinch to the spicy nose which fits perfectly with the dark brooding nature of the beast. The slightly singed toast acts as a perfect counter to the mint and orange rind. Really complex and tempting.

TASTE
Wow! Loads of everything, as you might expect from the nose. A deep, satin-smooth oak and burnt sugar backdrop allows the malt and rye to have a big say. Lots of vanilla, too.

FINISH
Here, as it dries, the corn comes into dominance. Some vanilla toffee, too.

COMMENTS
Magnificent stuff from Heaven Hill that really is worth hunting for.

J. W. DANT BIB • 100 PROOF

Not too bad a BIB, this. Limited complexity but just enough interesting things going on to make it worth investigating.

OLD BARDSTOWN BIB • 100 PROOF

NOSE
A heavyweight and a thoroughbred. Beautiful spice and apples teaming up with acacia honey sweetness. Delightful.

TASTE
A real mouthful that carries on the honied theme from the start and offers a good, firm rye character. Extremely oily and big in the mouth but all that with only limited oak.

FINISH
The oily character hangs around as does a little honey. A biscuity dryness announces the march of the barley and oak which intensifies for the best part of two minutes. Delicious.

COMMENTS
This whiskey has very little to do with either of the named Heaven Hill BIBs. This is even better than Dowling. For best and most consistent results try to find an old bottle still sealed - they are around in reasonable numbers.

LABROT AND GRAHAM

Just a couple of years back, anyone travelling along the old McCracken Mill Turnpike Road which leads eventually out of Frankfort and snakes its way southwards beside Glenns Creek, may have noticed a rather sad and sorry pile of buildings in a hollow to the right. Immediately they would have been recognizable as the remains of yet another fallen distillery. Four miles back, on the other side of the sprawling and charmingly backwooded hamlet of Millville you would have already had passed the abandoned Old Crow Distillery and just over half a mile further on the almost surreal site of the turreted Old Taylor distillery, silent for over a decade.

Today, that third distillery, then the most dilapidated of them all, is producing once more. Its renaissance represents one of the most astonishing tales in the already remarkable story of bourbon. This is the Labrot and Graham

distillery, which dates so far back into the infancy, if not conception, of organised Kentucky distilling that, like the legendary Cameronbridge distillery in Scotland, those connected with it read like a directory of the influential distillers of their nation.

The actual location of the distillery has as much to do with the revival of the L&G plant as anything. Back towards Millville and those other two famous distilleries there is some of the most spectacular and beautiful scenery to be found

Above

The Labrot and Graham distillery boasts an unrivalled bourbon-making pedigree.

anywhere in bourbon-making country. Either side of Glenns Creek the land lifts some 300 feet in no time at all. Coming in off these hills can be seen deer and wild turkey in abundance while the call of the coyote is never far away and vultures often circle overhead in search of a tasty morsel. Even in midwinter, when clouds are at their greyest and an eerie mist hangs over the babbling waters, birds send liquid and enchanting calls from one leafless branch to another. This may be only five miles from the state capital, but make no mistake: here you are in deepest, darkest and almost timeless Kentucky.

It was in the small flood plains that the distilleries and communities to serve them flourished. By the time you reach Labrot and Graham the steep hills have softened to the comparatively gentle, undulating and fertile lands for which the Blue Grass region is famed. Hereabouts thoroughbreds on the many horse farms can be seen, and sometimes even Queen Elizabeth II of England quietly inspecting her pride and joy in well-respected Kentuckian privacy.

During the 19th century the whiskies to be found along Glenns Creek were considered thoroughbreds, too. That was largely due to one man, James Crow (see Jim Beam, Old Crow). This greatly respected Scotsman, a physician by training, a chemist and distiller by heart, was greatly sought after by distillers and he spent his life perfecting though not, as is often claimed, inventing the sour mash method. Much of his work was carried out at L&G, a distillery he ran for some 20 years, back in the days when it was known as Oscar Pepper.

The Peppers were a highly influential distilling family. They left Virginia in around 1790 as the Culpepers (with a city and county named after them). Oscar's father Elijah changed their name and built a log cabin, which still stands today as one of the most remarkable remnants of early frontier life. This home was at the heart of the land he had bought for farming and on the other side of the creek he built a small distillery and then a larger and better one close to some excellent limestone springs, which was to become the Labrot and Graham distillery of today. This was Elijah's third distillery, having distilled in Virginia and already built a distillery with his brother-in-law in Versailles to the south.

After old Elijah's death, Oscar Pepper took control of the distillery and hired James Crow who had already made a reputation for himself first at Field's distillery further south in Woodford County at Griers Creek and then much closer to Peppers at the Henry Distillery also on Glenns Creek (or Glen's Creek as it was then known). From then on the land around Glenns Creek was to become home to Crow – the first man to remove by scientific exactitude many of the myriad uncertainties from distilling, using the same scientifically-based method as today. And there is no doubt that much of his greatest work was carried out at the old Pepper distillery, thereby making it one of the most historically significant distilleries anywhere in the world.

On a millstone above the distillery entrance can be seen in faded writing the words, Oscar Pepper Distillery, Est. 1838. This is rather confusing because it is unknown exactly what Oscar did at that time, whether he completely rebuilt the distillery in stone or simply changed its name. Or both. The distillery finally left the Pepper family in 1870 when James E. Pepper, who is believed to have taken over the distillery as a sixteen-year-old left to seek his fortune in New York, only to return a few years later as a bankrupt.

Above

An old bottle of Pepper bourbon, made by the family that built the Labrot and Graham distillery in 1838.

For the next eight years just about every big distilling name in the Frankfort area ran the distillery for a short while. They included Gains, who were to later build the Old Crow distillery, a bankrupt called Col. Edmund Taylor, who was to gain international fame when later building Old Taylor Distillery a few miles further down Glenns Creek and, finally, George T. Stagg who went on to own and gain recognition for what is now the Ancient Age distillery. Finally, in 1878, it was taken over by James Graham and Frenchman Leopold Labrot. The distillery continued under the auspices of Labrot and Graham until 1941, silent only during Prohibition.

The name was one of the most famous in America, though hardly anywhere outside, by the time Brown-Forman bought it for the paltry sum of just $75,000. Extraordinarily, that deal included not only the buildings and land, but no fewer than 25,673 barrels of top-grade bourbon. It was one of the best deals struck anywhere in the world's whiskey industry this century and helped Brown-Forman out of a hole: they had recently been operating at a loss and did not have sufficient whiskey stocks to cope with any upturn in demand. As Earl Dorsey was to later reflect: "We had to buy some whiskey or face a time when we had nothing to sell: that L&G whiskey put us back in business. It really saved this company." Even so, once it had served its purpose, its days were numbered. They closed it in 1970 when the demand for bourbon was taking an alarmingly downward spiral and many distilleries throughout the state were being regarded as surplus to requirements. After it fell silent the land was sold and the buildings and apparatus allowed to fall into decay. Even as late as 1995 I used to visit the

Above
Oscar Pepper lost control of the distillery when he was bankrupt in the 1870s.

distillery to take samples of the spent grains used in the final distillation which were still clogging the pipework.

Yet given the demand for small-batch bourbon rising during the 1990s, Brown-Forman made a remarkable move. After a state-wide search for the right place they bought back the lands and buildings – this time for a lot more than $75,000 – and after a 25-year enforced silence the Labrot and Graham distillery was back up to scratch, ready to distil again. The $10-million revamp included carefully preserving as many of the original limestone buildings as was possible, including the stunningly glorious and impressively solid distillery. Even more remarkable, they replaced the old and corroded distilling equipment with three brand new pot stills, made by the famed Scottish Highland stillmakers, Forsyths of Rothes. They even had seconded to them a Scottish distillery manager, Ed Dodson of Glen Moray (who was later to be instrumental in re-starting the famed Ardbeg distillery on Islay). Ed worked with the Brown-Forman staff at the Early Times distillery in Louisville in experiments to get the pot still distillation method, lost to Kentucky (since, ironically, the Old Crow distillery closed for Prohibition), back in harness. What made life difficult was the unusual, indeed truly unique method, of passing beer complete with solids into the first pot still.

But by July 1996 the problems had been overcome and the stills were transferred the 50 miles from Louisville to Labrot and Graham for the first distillation. The mashbill used was the traditional and greatly favoured Old Forester recipe of 72 per cent corn, 18 per cent rye and 10 per cent malted barley. They have also made small quantities from a second mashbill with greater corn, something akin to the Early Times recipe.

Particularly attractive are the fermenters, made of cypress wood and holding a meagre 7,500 gallons, dwarf-like compared to the metal fermenters which once served the old continuous

Left
A rare old L&G label from a now defunct brand.

165

stills there. The redundant warehouses, some of brick, some of stone, having survived the passage of time are today being filled once again. The spirit maturing in them is progressing confidently and healthily. Especially good is the maturing Forester recipe whiskey which is already showing delicate spices and fruit with soft vanillas and lingering rye. From the dozen or so samples I've tasted from the barrel, chances are, this, by the year 2001 when the first L&G whiskey is likely to be bottled, will prove to be a rich, oily and impressively intense bourbon for its age, a little spicy though not overly heavy. Only time, though, will tell.

Tales of this old distillery abound. From the distillery manager who accidentally lost a thumb whilst at work and buried it with full honours at the old cemetery opposite; to the distillery manager who in a cunning and none too humane plan to discover who was pilfering stocks, actually poisoned some whiskey to find who was too sick to work the following day. Even now it is a place where things just seems to happen, like a 10-foot long cow sucker snake being found in the distillery building by manager Dave Scheurich; a valve blowing like a discharged pistol during the first-ever distillation; the coolers to the fermenters being accidentally shut off in only their second time of operation, leaving the fermenting mash to bubble uncontrolled over the sides and on to the floor; the plant being forced into hasty closure and evacuation in March 1997 due to a foot of muddy water swimming through the distillery during the worst floods in living memory.

But not even the forces of nature could prevent Labrot and Graham becoming the showpiece distillery of Kentucky, now officially recognized by the government by being placed on the National Historic Registry. A visitor centre has been built to accommodate the expected 100,000 visitors each year, and, like the new distillery manager's house, was painstakingly designed to blend in with the elegant and traditional style of the homes of the area.

Labrot and Graham is not just a success story for a distilling nation but the whiskey world in general. It shows, in no uncertain terms, just what can be achieved when an appreciation of culture and tradition is writ larger than an accountant's bottom line. And for a whiskey writer who has seen more dead and dying distilleries worldwide than an ever-saddening heart can bear, it is the cleanest breath of fresh air that can ever be drawn; the purest injection of joy and hope.

Dreams, so it seems, do come true. And the impossible can happen. Kentucky, is indeed, a truly remarkable land.

WOODFORD RESERVE • 90.4 PROOF

Named after the county in which the L&G distillery is located, this is whisky distilled at Early Times to the high rye Old Forester recipe. The barrels had finished their maturation at L&G, hence the connection with the distillery. The whisky is aged for between 6.5 and 7.5 years.

NOSE One of the gentlest of all Kentucky's bourbons. Remarkable cream toffee with sweet vanilla. Of the very simple yet enticing variety.

TASTE A gossamer light entrance on the palate followed by a nutty dryness and echoes of sweet corn.

FINISH The rye begins to harden up on the finale as a little warming spice but there is also a cocoa-like bitterness. Very late oak sees the whiskey off.

COMMENTS This is a charming, though ultimately very simplistic, bourbon from the Old Forester stable of the Early Times distillery. There are little hints of its association, mainly through the rye and pepper, but otherwise it is far removed. The caramel-toffee is easily the most dominant character and guarantees an exceptionally smooth bourbon throughout. Impressively refined.

PRESIDENT'S RESERVE
100.4 PROOF

A rarer brand bottled at 100.4 proof, the whiskey is otherwise the same as Woodford Reserve, having been "finished" in the upper tiers of the Labrot and Graham warehouses. The barrels selected for Presidents Reserve are those boasting bourbon of a darker colour and richer character. A pleasant whiskey, but not a patch on the surprisingly delicate Woodford Reserve or even Forester '96. Complex and moreish, but just not quite enough lingering sweetness to make for a truly great whiskey.

MAKER'S MARK

Sunset in Kentucky can sometimes leave you spellbound and by strange coincidence two of the best I have seen have been in a hollow by a creek in the southernmost outpost of the distilling region.

That was at Maker's Mark, a distillery of farm-like proportions found a few miles east of Loretto. As the sun sets amongst the small hills enveloping the distillery the golden fingers stretching from the sky down on to the distillery buildings seem to reflect the maturing whiskies inside those padlocked old barns.

While the distilleries of Glenns Creek are situated in land that would be instantly recognisable to the first explorers of these parts, the softly sculpted pastures in which Maker's Mark stands are exactly what those first settlers dreamed their new country would become.

Maybe, then, it is no coincidence that Maker's Mark has become something of a cult whisky. Tourists and whisky lovers who go there seem to have a habit of making their way back, or staying loyal to the brand influenced jointly by the persuasive charms of the whisky and by the effect that the visit has had upon them. And it has helped that the distillery, though so small, is part

of one of the world's most enormous spirit concerns, Allied Domecq. They have been instrumental in making it available in outlets around the world where bourbons have previously had a problem getting a toe-hold.

But the ace it held up its sleeve was allowing the distillery to go its own merry way, leaving Bill Samuels, the son of the founder, and bourbon activist of immense energy and pride, in charge and making sure that it never lost that truly Old Kentucky Home feel. High international demand for the whisky has meant pressure has been brought to bear over recent years in upping production, not an easy thing to do. Firstly, there has not been enough water to go around, the nightmare of any distillery. And secondly, once you change the design of the stills in order to produce more, the quality of the whisky will

Above
Though of quaint farm-like proportions, Maker's Mark produces a big rye-free whiskey.

change – though it is in the lap of the gods as to whether it will be for better or worse. Chances are it will not be for the better.

Yet Maker's Mark is in the unusual and envious position of having such welcome headaches. Just about every other distillery is underproducing. So some time after the turn of the millennium a second distillery will be built behind the first, one change being that they will install metal fermenters rather than wooden ones: already as a concession to increased demand they have employed extra stainless steel fermenters, but only after undertaking extensive experimentation over years to discover that fermentation in wood or metal made no discernible change to their final product. Without doubt though, the wooden fermenters in place help make Maker's Mark one of the most picturesque, internally as well as externally, in all America.

But there is no taking away from the polished glory of the stillroom, either, where the short, copper continuous stills add an air of elegance while on a floor below the copper doubler ensures a rich finish to the emerging spirit.

The Star Hill Distillery, to give it its proper name, dates all the way back to the first decade of the 19th century, and by the time Bill's father, William, decided to re-enter the bourbon industry in 1954, it was virtually on its last legs. Samuels has long been one of the most famous names in Kentucky distilling, with a town named after the family that entered Kentucky at the turn of the 19th century having started out as Pennsylvanian distillers. In the nearby town of Deatsville can still be seen the buildings of the first Samuels distillery, dating back to the mid-19th century, and when the plush Dining Train from Bardstown passes by on warm summer evenings diners can, if the wind is in the right direction, enjoy the aroma of maturing Maker's Mark whisky wafting from the warehouses which remain in use.

When William Samuels decided to rebuild and rename the Happy Hollow Distillery Star Hill, he also decided that the character of the whisky should be somewhat different. On the advice of Pappy Van Winkle of Stitzel Weller he decided upon dispensing with rye and adding wheat as a flavouring ingredient, (strange for the descendant of a Pennsylvanian distiller) and they have continued with that formula to this day with 14 per cent wheat to 16 per cent malted barley. Also because of the relatively small batch whisky being made the unique policy has been to use barrels which have enjoyed year-long full open-aired seasoning to soften the effect the virgin oak will have on the spirit. When the distillery begins to double its output this might prove a very expensive procedure.

Even the bottling is different. The labels are hand made in a small workshop at the distillery and each bottle is hand dipped in a plastic-wax

Above
Adding the
brand's
distinctive
wax seal.

fondue that dries leaving an individually shaped seal on each bottle. It all amounts to an above average price, but it remains a big seller in Kentucky none the less.

Hopefully the new extension will do nothing to subtract from the charm of the little distillery built beside Hardin's Creek and over a tributary to it that Clint Eastwood would admire – it's a creek with no name. Already some extension has taken place, but you would barely know it: a new building has been erected for filling the barrels, and has been designed in the style of a turn of the century warehouse and painted in the same black and red livery which so easily identifies the distillery. Plans have already been made to make better use of limited spring water by using it exclusively for mashing. And they have even made a deal with the Catholic nuns of the Order of Loretto to produce all the extra wheat they need. Indeed, barley apart, all the grain used for distilling is as local as they can get it.

History abounds at Maker's Mark. It has even officially become a national monument, a bit like Bill Samuels who continued the strong Kentucky line by marrying a descendant of Daniel Boone. In an office at the distillery there are even the guns which once belonged to Jesse and Frank James who were related to him and were protected by the sheriff who also happened to have been one of Bill's great uncles.

When many years ago Bill first told me about all this – and the history and beauty of his distillery – I found it all rather hard to believe and felt tempted to sprinkle an extra pinch of salt on to my dinner. Nothing, surely, could be that romantic. Well, actually it can...

Left
Idyllic surrounding pastures combine with the building's distinctive red and black livery to create Kentucky's most attractive distillery.

MAKER'S MARK • 66-MONTH-OLD • 90 PROOF

NOSE Moderate hints of honey, sunflower seeds, malt and dry oak all in a slightly creamy, oily texture. Magnificent.

TASTE Very firm start on the palate, hard even. Then softens as there is a rush of buttery corn sweetness and teasing peppery notes.

FINISH Amazingly long, complex and rich. The peppers form a perfect background to the cream toffee sweetness which takes command. A slight liquorice toasty oakiness hangs on for the very finale.

COMMENTS This is magnificent whisky throughout. Because this is a pretty small batch distillery there are some differences to be found in samples from time to time. Some older Maker's Mark I have bottled at this age age reveals a greater honey profile, others a lot more rich, ripe fruit to add to the corn sweetness. Even so, all this falls into a pattern and style unique to Maker's Mark. Also, the pepperiness is a giveaway of the wheat presence. No two bottles are ever quite the same, it seems to me. But nor could they be mistaken for anything else.

MAKER'S MARK • 95 PROOF

NOSE Genuine honey here; not just a hint. Shades of kiwi fruit and ripe plums. Something approaching the intensity of a rich fruit cake but the sweetness stems from the corn rather than sugar.

TASTE The bourbon immediately envelopes the mouth in oil of hazelnut and strong malt. Lots of toffee and vanilla arrive from the ultra-smooth middle.

FINISH There oak gathers pace but never quite manages to match the heaviness of the younger Maker's Marks. The most lasting effect is the cream caramel and just a hint of grainy ripeness.

COMMENTS This is an outstanding whisky, an absolute must for those who prefer their bourbon to show great poise and smoothness. The spices have just about been aged out of it and the pepper attack, always expected with Maker's, never gets through. A glorious bourbon to savour in some of the quieter moments in life.

MAKER'S MARK • 101 PROOF

NOSE Similar to the 90 proof but more burnt toast and deeper cooked blackberries. The oak is a little more forceful though the peppers and oils remain constant.

TASTE Much sweeter, more intense start with the corn hitting the palate running. The oil is a tad thicker and lines the mouth well. The peppers, despite the strength are more docile.

FINISH Longer, oilier and sweeter: not so much from the corn but more molasses. Not quite so weighty as the 90 proof.

COMMENTS Where the 90 proof starts light and becomes heavier this works in exactly the opposite way. Still wonderfully industrious on the palate and the intensity is breathtaking.

1983 VINTAGE BOURBON • 95 PROOF

NOSE This is as good as Maker's Mark gets. The tell-tale maker's honey character is here with depth and this mingles luxuriously with toffee caramel and oranges. Lots of other fruits abound, too. Excellent.

TASTE Soft and silky with an immediate spice presence (the wheat?). The malt makes its mark and the oiliness sticks lovingly to the palate to guarantee a big middle.

FINISH Amazingly long and subtle. This is like the long dying rays of the sun going down with a golden beauty. The honey has returned but has alongside it a caramel and nut richness. The oak is also present here but in exactly the right amount. Stupendous.

COMMENTS This is the pick of the Maker's Mark range and one of the top five bourbons I've ever tasted. The balance is astonishing, as is its complexity. A whisky which, should you ignore it on the shelf, you may regret it for ever.

MEDLEY

The Medley distillery in Owensboro has undergone a chequered career of late and is currently silent. It was recently in the hands of Glenmore Distillers who re-opened the plant in 1991 only for new owners United Distillers to close it down again in early 1992. It is now owned by Charles Medley, who has long hankered after restarting his old family concern. Original Medley whiskey is used in his Wathen brand which, sadly is not one of the finest you will find: classic "start-up whiskey". A rye bottled by Van Winkle (see rye) is a much better proposition. There would be nothing better, though, than seeing the distillery up and running again and this time given a chance to show what it can do.

WATHEN'S • 94 PROOF (Barrel No.3, bottled 1-29-97.)

Henry Hudson Wathen was one of the first distillers in Kentucky, from a family that married into the Medleys. Charles Medley's middle name is Wathen. The Wathen's distilling tradition died out after Prohibition. The whiskey was matured in small two-storey high brick warehouses. Distilled by Glenmore, it would have been made for either Yellowstone, Kentucky Tavern or Ezra Brooks brands. Apart from a few seconds when a classic, sweet bourbon richness battles through this is a whiskey that refuses to get into shape and the off-notes dominate. While the taste may be harsh the nose is rather lovely. Hopefully a few extra years will straighten this whiskey out.

STITZEL WELLER

For a little while it looked as though the proud old Stitzel Weller distillery in Louisville might just be saved. Certainly there was no chance of it ever being brought back to life in its full capacity as when the famous Old Fitzpatrick and Weller brands were made there. But there were plans afoot, even if only in early discussion stages, to make it a small batch plant with tiny copper pots. It would never have been perfect - Stitz is the kind of distillery that gives the feeling of grandiose dimensions, everything big and beautiful - but it would have been a welcome substitute for watching the place disintegrate.

Those hopes looked dashed when owners United Distillers linked with IDV. But should they sell Bernheim to Heaven Hill, the Stitzel Weller distillery might be brought back to full capacity. But at the moment it is only a possibility. I can but pray, because although found within city environs, Stitzel Weller is an elegant distillery exuding class. The old stack proudly displays Old Fitzgerald in a tradition now lost. And it is surrounded by fabulous ironclad warehousing, where even now the wheated bourbon made at Bernheim continues to be stored.

Above
Warehouses and
cooper's shop at
the Stitzel Weller
distillery.

The Old Fitzgerald brand made at Stitzel Weller was a classic when allowed to mature. At too young an age it almost bordered on the unpleasant and regular Old Fitz would be one of the last bourbons I would ever choose. Which is odd, because once it begins to take colour then it becomes one of my first, especially the 12-year-old Very Old Fitzgerald.

However, there was one younger wheated bourbon made there which I do appreciate, Rebel Yell, a busy delicately spiced whiskey. For generations a whiskey sold only in confederate states it was marketed internationally, and with dire results. The distillery overproduced as the demand for the whiskey never materialised and the future of the plant was placed in jeopardy.

Stitzel Weller came about after two smallish

established distillers - W.L. Weller, who date back to 1849, and the Stitzel Distilling Co. (1870) - merged during Prohibition. The distillery dates back to 1935 but somehow seems older. The Old Fitzgerald brand came from another distillery which also closed during Prohibition, the Old Fitzgerald distillery of Frankfort. The man behind its revival was the legendary owner Julian "Pappy" Van Winkle who put a sign up outside his office declaring what he thought of unnatural methods for making bourbon: "No Chemists Allowed." It was rather ironic, then, that the company had during Prohibition gained a licence to sell their whiskey for medicinal purposes.

Today his grandson Julian Van Winkle keeps the family name going with his quite excellent Pappy Van Winkle brand which is, fittingly, from

Above
A turn-of-the-century Old Fitzgerald ad.

Above
The legendary Julian "Pappy" Van Winkle gives thanks that his distillery is a chemist-free zone.

predominantly Stitzel Weller stock. However, he has no plans to buy the silent old distillery as it is too big for his needs. The one bourbon diversion he made was to pick up some old whiskey from the Boone distillery which he marketed as a 20-year-old. It won a medal, but was by far the worst whiskey he has bottled. But as the Stitzel Weller distillery has learnt to its cost, quality does not always lead to the rewards it deserves.

184

W. L. WELLER ANTIQUE • 107 PROOF

NOSE Wet carpets? Highly distinctive certainly unlike any other bourbon. There are figs and ripe dates in there somewhere, too. Fascinating and very attractive.

TASTE Wow! A massive start, absolutely exploding all over the taste-buds with fat, oaky notes but nothing too heavy. There is rich corn present as the middle formulates with demerara sugar and traces of treacle cake.

FINISH Big, thundering vanilla shows the oak is having a big say, but there is sufficient corn and small grain present to demand complexity. Chewy and formidable.

COMMENTS Highly impressive stuff. One of the biggest, if not the biggest, wheat recipe bourbons you will ever find. Initially not for the squeamish as you need taste-buds that can ride this. But it is ultimately calm and stable. Magnificent.

W. L. WELLER CENTENNIAL 10-YEAR-OLD 100 PROOF

NOSE Seems younger. Some youthful, greenish small grain notes hold the attention as the encroaching oaky vanillas look on.

TASTE Ah! Delicate stuff. Again it is the small grains, the barley and wheat, which arrive first on the palate and are very light and flighty. The middle sweetens and fattens out as some deep liquorice-toffee arrives.

FINISH Slightly peppery beginnings and a gradual build up of

oak, too. The mouth is hotting up under this barrage. Still delicate and toffee sweet, but much more aggressive in character thanks to this influx of spices.

COMMENTS What a complex whiskey. Refuses to sit still at any time. Wheat bourbons tend towards a spicy character and this one goes the whole way. Great stuff. And not least because it hangs on to a rich sweetness almost until the last. Required drinking for its genre.

W. L. WELLER SPECIAL RESERVE • 90 PROOF

Somewhat lacking in character, this is another wheated bourbon which suffers from youth. After the pleasant first ten seconds on arrival it goes rapidly downhill.

OLD FITZGERALD • 86 PROOF

This is a wheated bourbon which are temperamental beasts. It does not appear to have quite matured as long as it wished. A straight up-and-downer with basic toffee. There are one or two pleasant phases, but ultimately unsatisfying.

OLD FITZGERALD BIB 100 PROOF

NOSE Slightly creamier toffee. Shades of butter, perhaps. Surprisingly less spicy than the ordinary Old Fitz.

TASTE Sweeter, more intense start and much more oily. The middle soon becomes rather bland, though, with corn the most dominant.

FINISH Drier, oilier and still the corn hangs on. There is something slightly hard and metallic trying to arrive at the very finish. Slightly disjointed.

COMMENTS A great improvement on the 86 proof simply because the sweetness and oiliness cover the bitterness almost entirely. A good session whiskey, providing you are not looking for something of great finesse.

OLD FITZGERALD 1849 • 8-YEAR-OLD • 90 PROOF

NOSE Ethereal and slightly spirity. Some very hard green malty notes gives the impression that it is younger than its real age. Attractive, even so.

TASTE Very sweet and crisp arrival on the palate. The wheat is more noticeable at this particular age than any other and boasts some of the banana characteristics sometimes found in wheat beer. A very refreshing, mildly citrusy mouth-feel.

FINISH Tang of lemon with vague oak and soft toffees.

COMMENTS A very unusual bourbon, and quite different from other Old Fitz brands. This is probably my favourite of them all, especially on days when you just want to relax. Older Fitz have more power and complexity. This has excellent balance.

OLD RIP VAN WINKLE • 10-YEAR-OLD 107 PROOF

With mango and banana on the nose you know you are in for something a little special and the peppered toffee reveals enormous quality. More of a box of tricks than the lower proof version with a more satisfying finish. Some expressions of this whiskey have been simply outstanding and it is very similar in its dazzling intensity to the 15-year-old. The 90 proof bottling is a subtler yet somehow less impressive version.

OLD RIP VAN WINKLE • 15-YEAR-OLD • 107 PROOF

This whiskey supplied to Julian Van Winkle is the only wheated bourbon sold by IDV to an outside company. Yet with the advent of a new marketing strategy within the company, the days of this whiskey under this particular label may be numbered.

NOSE Simply enormous. A massive dose of oak knocks your senses off balance for a second or two. The richness is akin to a moist fruitcake, so profound are the raisins. Softer vanillas, too. Stunning

TASTE Extraordinary density in the mouth, a whiskey you really can chew. It has the sweetness of a greatly aged Jamaican rum and much of the oiliness as well. Just a little of the tell-tale wheat-recipe spice but heaps of malted barley.

FINISH Long with lots of raisin fruit, dark sugar and corn. The oak presence adds an extra weighty dimension, but is not even slightly too intense.

COMMENTS Pretty close to perfection. It has to be said that this whiskey has an enormous similarity in style to Wild Turkey 12-year-old, though one is wheat and the other rye. In a blind tasting you would find it hard to choose and they are almost interchangeable. Curious, puzzling but ultimately highly delicious. A classic which shows just what an immeasurable loss the Stitzel Weller distillery has been to Kentucky and bourbon drinkers.

OLD RIP VAN WINKLE SPECIAL RESERVE
12-YEAR-OLD • 90.4 PROOF

Maple syrup and sweet corn form the unlikely combination that underpins the character of this whiskey. What a pleasant whiskey; a kind of well-mannered old gentleman whom you cannot help but like. The finish is rather shallow, but forget that. The nose is class and something you are likely only to find amongst wheated bourbons. Not in the same league as the 10-year-old 107 but this does have some deeply satisfying moments.

PAPPY VAN WINKLE'S FAMILY RESERVE
20-YEAR-OLD • 90.4 PROOF
(From the Boone Dist.)

NOSE Past its sell-by date. The oak has taken too great a grip, flat and unexciting. Just a hint of honey and marzipan redeems it a little but the menthol effect is a pointer towards the oak having gotten out of hand. (At its best when nosed from empty overnight glass.)

TASTE Over-woody to the point of being sappy. Even the last remnants of sweetness cannot save this one as the honey goes it alone amid the chewy pencil ends.

FINISH Dry and characterless.

COMMENTS In 1997 this won a Platinum Medal in the World Spirits Championships, held by the Beverage Testing Institute of Chicago. It actually rated a mind-busting 99 points out of a 100, thereby announcing this whiskey as close to perfection as you can get. Either they were sampling something totally different from the three Pappys I have now tasted or the judges were having an off day. Come on, guys, get real. In the thousands of tastings I have conducted either privately or for various competitions I have never rated any whiskey higher than 94, and I must have tasted just about the lot. The stupendous 15-year-old Old Rip was judged far more accurately, probably deserving something in the 90s, though the 97 is still stretching it a bit. I very rarely reveal my own marks for every individual whiskey. But in this case I will let you into the secret that my score (originally blind-tasted) for Pappy was: nose 10/20; taste 5/15; finish 4/15 — a total of 21/50.

REBEL YELL • 80 PROOF

NOSE An extraordinary nose, full of peppers on the warpath. There is a big vanilla kick as well and sweet corn oil. In the background is something dusty and dry but by no means unpleasant.

TASTE One of the most complex starts from the distillery. In the first few seconds there is a sweet-dry-sweet interchange with some apple and orange briefly adding a mouthwatering quality. This disappears quickly to be finally replaced by dry oak.

FINISH There is a peppery fix throughout the finish and very dry oak.

COMMENTS Great whiskey. Non-stop action in the mouth leaves your taste-buds exhausted. Not quite as crisp as I once remembered it but no less complex and warming!

RX BOURBON

A recent launch of a brand that is geared to the younger market as it does not use the word whiskey at all. The label confusingly gives the George Dickel signature across the 6-year age statement and announces the Tennessee address as well. It even makes the point of the whiskey having been filtered through sugar maple. But this is not Tennessee, this is Kentucky bourbon distilled at Stitz. This is not mentioned anywhere but the RX is a clue. It was a name given to whiskey sold on prescription during Prohibition and Dickel did move to Kentucky during that time. The bourbon itself is not at all bad, one of the sweetest on the market with the filtration process obviously having something to do with that. The softness allows the taste-buds to concentrate on the delicate vanillas, wheat...and maple syrup. A genteel, unbelievably moreish, whiskey offering not a scrap of complexity but as easy-going as it gets. Mind you, had it been the real Prohibition stuff it would have been 100 proof and a slightly different story...

VERY SPECIAL OLD FITZGERALD • 12-YEAR-OLD 90 PROOF

NOSE This is a different ball-game. Massive complexity with shades of unripe green bananas, sandalwood, malt, soft ground peppers and raisins. Even shades of applejack. Stunning.

TASTE Bittersweet start. Enormous complexity from the off with creamy oils forming the backdrop to a bitter-vanilla middle. Sweet custardy notes are also about.

FINISH Medium to long and quite dry. There is some toffee-fudge but this disappears to leave more vanilla and gentle oak.

COMMENTS A surprise package in that the nose suggests it to be sweeter and deeper than it actually is. Having said that, this is a superb bourbon simply because each time you taste it, it registers a slightly different character. A bourbon you can never quite get the bottom of. Doubtless, it will be less challenging to get to the bottom of the bottle.

WILD TURKEY

The neat and tidy town of Lawrenceburg, about 15 miles south of Frankfort, is home to some the most impressive residences in all Anderson County. Some were built from the profits of the many distilleries that flourished in those parts during the 18th and early 19th centuries. None of these distilleries was in the town itself. But many were located in a town called Tyrone on the banks of the Kentucky river and blessed with a bounty of clear, limestone springs.

While Lawrenceburg has prospered, Tyrone once boasting a population of some 600 souls, has all but vanished. There is nothing more to find than a quarry and a few farm buildings, the homes of tobacco growers. It is under this crop that the remains of some of these old distilleries lie today.

But one distillery has survived, just a few feet west of the old Tyrone border and a minute or two by car from Lawrenceburg. Originally it was the Ripy distillery, named after one of the first families ever to settle the area. Today it is known throughout the world as the Wild Turkey distillery.

Most Kentucky distilleries are beautifully situated: Labrot and Graham, Jim Beam and

Four Roses are all found in stunning countryside and Ancient Age by the old Kentucky river. Wild Turkey adds a further dimension: drama. It, too, is beside the Kentucky, but you would have to endure a sheer, 259-foot drop to reach it. The distillery in its livery of drab brown guards the river like an old castle and its precarious position is highlighted by the rotting remains of a single-track railroad bridge that fords the gorge the third of a mile to the opposite bank. The trestled construction once supported the locos which shunted grain into the distillery. Trains still come and go, parking directly outside the entrance to the still house, but now take the safer route through Lawrenceburg.

Of all the continuous still bourbon distilleries, this is the most impressive to view. Many of the

Above

The Wild Turkey distillery sits on a high gorge above the Kentucky river like a Rhine castle.

fermenters, in which a mash of 75 per cent corn 12 per cent rye and 13 per cent malt bubbles away, are still made of cypress wood, having outlasted those at neighbouring Four Roses. They help to give the place a feeling of age and timelessness and soften what in other distilleries can be a visually harsh environment. So, too, does the wonderful all-copper beer still. Even the lovely old doubler, also of gleaming copper, adds to the sense of long ago.

Yet in fact the distillery has only been known as Wild Turkey since 1971. Before then it was the old JTS Brown distillery, which had been making whiskey under contract for the Wild Turkey brand for a great many years. Indeed, the 1855 date given to one of the Wild Turkey brands, does not actually represent when the distillery was built, which was exactly 50 years later when three Ripy brothers decided to go it alone from their father's plant a mile or two down the hill at Tyrone. In fact, 1855 refers to when the Austin Nichol Company was formed as importers of, amongst other things, spirits. They had specialized for many years in Scotch and Irish but during World War II the company decided to concentrate more on bourbon, which was not only easier to get, but the preferred choice of the then owner, Thomas McCarthy. In 1942 he christened his 8-year-old 101 proof brand Wild Turkey and bought stocks from various Kentucky distillers until in the end it was JTS

Brown who produced most of the product. Today the distillery is in the control of the French beverage company Pernod Ricard.

Tradition stills plays an important part in daily life at Wild Turkey. Just as Elmer T Lee learned from a Blanton, the founding family at Ancient Age, so distillery manager Jimmy Russell in his 40-odd years at the plant once worked for a Ripy. And when Jimmy retires (quite soon now) it will be his son taking over the reins. Jimmy has always preferred bourbon to be bottled at 101 proof and Wild Turkey make a special point of doing that. Even the excellent rye, which they make once a year there, is bottled at that strength.

To enjoy the whiskey at its finest it is worth paying a little over the odds. When young it is good but there are other bourbons to match it. However, by the time it has hit 8-12 years it has taken on a honeyed intensity that no other bourbon can quite match. This is, quite simply, classic stuff.

When people ask me to name what I consider to be the three best whiskies to be made anywhere in the world, Wild Turkey, along with Ardbeg in Scotland and Ancient Age are my choices. And I cheerfully dare anyone to trump that.

WILD TURKEY • 80 PROOF

A firm but fresh whiskey, slightly astringent on the nose but with a sweetness of promise. Good but uninspiring whiskey.

WILD TURKEY • 12-YEAR-OLD • 101 PROOF

NOSE An incredible aroma of freshly peeled orange, acacia honey, crushed walnuts, raisins, molasses, rye, Indian corn oil, malted barley and very soft oak. One of the world's classic noses and unrivalled by any in Kentucky.

TASTE The kaleidoscopic qualities of the nose are translated directly on to the palate. There are a myriad breathtaking qualities, once the initial oak-heavy start has been overcome. The middle has plenty of gentle rye, sweet toffee and treacle.

FINISH Very soft and medium length. Breathtakingly delicate for a bourbon of this age. There is a wonderful sweet and sour battle going on between the dry oak and sweet caramel. The sweetness wins and more fruity raisin notes follow on with dried dates. Magnificent.

COMMENTS As complex as the taste of this whiskey is, it still cannot match the extraordinary nose. This is not so fulfilling as the better of their single barrel 8-year-olds, but as a vatted bourbon it is probably my favourite. Glorious.

WILD TURKEY OLD NO.8 BRAND • 86.8 PROOF
This the European version which just isn't a patch on the original 101.

NOSE Vaguely spearminty with sweet toffee. Extremely light, teasing almost.

TASTE Full and bracing at first, then the mintiness and a little maltiness pull through before a very oily corn cereal centre arrives.

FINISH Medium length, hints of menthol and much more oak to dry it out. Some delicious rye arrives at the very end to add a fruity bite.

COMMENTS A sound, confident bourbon with pleasing complexity that uses its small grains cleverly to add that extra degree of richness.

WILD TURKEY OLD NO. 8 BRAND • 101 PROOF

NOSE Fuller, fatter, excellent oak weight and a hint of brine.

TASTE Big and muscular. Enormous vanilla explosion as it enters the mouth with a short-lived flash of honey that makes for some cookie, cereal notes.

FINISH Here the honeycomb returns with a vengeance. Long and deep; given enough time you will spot dates, rich Dundee fruit cake, coconut, demerara sugar, rye and probably anything else you might care to mention.

COMMENTS A classic amongst everyday brands in the US. The day it was withdrawn from Europe was one of the saddest in recent years. A magnificent, classic, mega-complex whiskey with teeth.

WILD TURKEY RARE BREED/
WILD TURKEY 1855 RESERVE
110 PROOF
Rare Breed is the name used in the USA and export markets.1855 Reserve is the name given in the Duty Free market.

NOSE Prickly fresh, with layers of honey and dates.

TASTE Big arrival on the mouth, as one would expect at this strength. But still a very smooth, rich ride with a distinct oaky dryness thumping it out with a sweeter, molasses and faintly honeyed middle.

FINISH Only here does the corn and then rye notes begin to show. Amazingly delicate and refined finish following the battle that has been waged before. Superb.

COMMENTS A bourbon for those who prefer their steaks rare. Magnificent stuff, a tidal wave of pulsating flavours which are never less than full-bodied but always in magnificent harmony. One of the greatest whiskies in the world.

WILD TURKEY TRADITION • 101 PROOF

NOSE Honeydew melon, traces of hickory smoke and rye. Rather heavy with some pleasant oak.

TASTE Dry, oaky start then some white pepper spice and a gradual build up of sweet corn.

FINISH Oily to start, some cream- then treacle-toffee. This is easily the best part and remains sweet and chewy for a long time towards the very end taking on the character of Belgian honey waffles.

COMMENTS A bourbon that just gets better the longer you hold it in the mouth. An outstanding finish that builds up facet by facet into something very special.

KENTUCKY LEGEND SINGLE BARREL • 115.2 PROOF

NOSE Enormous honey, rich vanilla with faint rye and malt adding to the beauty.

TASTE Dry oak at first then an immense arrival of rich honey, treacle and liquorice all kept in place by a rye firmness.

FINISH Amazing long and luxurious. The honey and treacle hang on, the vanilla is no more than a soft shadow and the small grains weave small magic circles around the palate.

COMMENTS This is absolutely stunning stuff. This ranks in the top ten whiskies of all the tens of thousands it has been my pleasure and honour to taste. If anyone didn't believe me when I wrote a few years back that Wild Turkey is the classic of all bourbons, they should try this. Then I would like to hear their argument. As close to perfection in a glass as you are likely to find. And don't dare add water or ice.

KENTUCKY SPIRIT
SINGLE BARREL
101 PROOF

NOSE Fresh, minty, distinct aroma of oranges and rye.

TASTE Oaky and dry on introduction, then marmalade-sharp Seville orange. More cream toffee fills in towards the middle but some spirity burn reveals this as not quite so heavy in character as one might expect.

FINISH Medium length and sweet with delicious caramel toffee and corn. Pretty dry finish.

COMMENTS Quite a complex whiskey with powerful toffee and lacking the treacle-honey richness which sets the finest Wild Turkeys apart. That said, it is still majestic.

WILLETT

The Willett distillery sits back from the road from Bardstown to Loretto and may one day be back in production. Having survived being almost too close to the Heaven Hill fire for comfort, one hopes that their being spared was a sign from above that the distillery is destined to figure once more as a bourbon producer. You might find two whiskies from the original, now dismantled old Willett distillery. One is the far too old Noah's Mill, the other the astonishingly complex Johnny Drum which at 15 years is a celebration of small grain. Stocks are so low, apparently, that I cannot guarantee that the original Willett whiskey will be in there if you find it. But you never know.

GEORGIA WHISKEY

In the summer of 1997 Georgian bourbon was back in business. There had been two distilleries operating in the state, the Atlanta distillery and the Viking Distillery in Albany, just an hour from the Florida border. But they had been silent for a number of years.

The Atlanta distillery has all but gone now, all the distilling apparatus stripped away. The buildings still stand in pleasantly wooded lands just on the outskirts of the city.

The whiskey of the Viking distillery is made to an unusual 85 per cent corn 15 per cent rye mashbill with alpha enzymes, those extracted from malted barley being used to make fermentation possible. The distillery is an old, rather charming affair, the highlight being the fermentation room which includes eight aged, time-beaten old cypress fermenters which as well as looking after the bourbon are also pressed into active service for the making of the grain neutral spirit which goes into the Barton blends and also for famous old Georgia corn whiskey, the clear variety.

The distillery passed into the hands of Barton in 1995 after having been part of Glenmore and then United Distillers but did not begin distilling bourbon again until 1997. The bourbon is passed

through only a beer still, making it, like Jack Daniel's, unusual for being a single distillation product.

The whiskey is not bottled as a straight bourbon, though goes into various blends. At six years old, however, it proves to be a very sweet bourbon to nose, surprisingly so; slightly buttery but also with a deliciously attractive rye fruitiness. It is no less disappointing to taste; a bit hot perhaps but the flavour level is unusually intense. Again it is sweet but the rye adds a fatness which lets it stick around for a long time. The finish is soft with excellent oak balance and powering rye follow-through. This is a distinctive, confident bourbon deserving of its own brand, being quietly distinguished and full of flavour. It was certainly the biggest surprise I got on my journey around all of America's distilleries. And probably the most pleasant.

Above
After a considerable break Georgia whiskey is being made once again at the Viking distillery.

INDIANA WHISKEY

When you consider how few bourbon distilleries there are throughout North America, it's hard to believe that Indiana's one distillery is based in a town which shares the name of its sister distillery's town in Kentucky. The Indiana plant owned by Seagram is in Lawrenceburg, located east of Cincinnati beside the Ohio river, in lands as flat as those of its namesake Kentucky city are undulating. And where the neo-Spanish Four Roses is a veritable indulgence in distillery architecture, the Indiana plant is based in a solid boxed brick construction of little or no imagination.

There were other whiskey distilleries once in Lawrenceburg, notably Schenley's. But they are silent now. And for a short but depressing while, so too was Seagram's Indiana outpost, which dates back to 1865 (at least as a whiskey distillery anyway, as it makes vodka, gin and the grain neutral spirit for Seagram blends). The idea was to transfer whiskey production to Four Roses. But Indiana re-opened for business in February 1997 and deservedly so. For me, this makes the better whiskey of the two distilleries, though its only straight bourbon, Cougar, is shipped off to Australasia. The most full-flavoured, taste-bud devouring bourbon I have ever tasted came from here, boasting an eye-watering 35 per cent rye. Sadly it has never been marketed as a straight. They also make a more orthodox bourbon, too. Also made here was an all barley spirit which is matured into a flavouring component for their Seven Crown blend. Lawrenceburg's speciality is rye: first a stirring, truly magnificent sweetly spiced all malted rye affair which left the taste-buds quivering; one a little less voluptuous with 95 per cent unmalted rye to 5 per cent malted rye and finally a much more delicate and traditional 52 per cent rye effort. Again, sadly, all these were used for flavourings for blended and Canadian whiskey and none ever saw the light of day as a straight.

Some of us still remember an odd product called No. 1 Bourbon Street launched by Seagram in the early 90s which sank soon after without a trace. That was Indiana whiskey, though for some peculiar reason the label only said that it was a blend of the "Old New Orleans Style", whatever that meant. Yet it just didn't work on the palate despite consisting of 25 per cent straight rye. One that does work though is Sam Cougar, marketed only in Australasia, yet one of my favourite bourbons. Made from 75 per cent corn, 20 per cent rye and 5 per cent malt, it is about as tenacious a whiskey as you are likely to find, never letting go of the taste-buds once it gets hold of them. Flying to Australia can be relatively cheap these days. The fact you can drink Sam Cougar in the bargain makes it a steal.

SAM COUGAR BLACK • 74 PROOF

NOSE Wonderful nose where the rye makes a grand entrance with sweet malt not that far behind. Fruity and spicy with a touch of banana to soften it up a little. Really sturdy and rigid and amazingly appealing.

TASTE The rye is there for the hard yet beautifully tailored arrival. Some sweetcorn and mixed oils act as a brilliant lubricant on the mouth. There are tangy rye, raisin and citrus notes. So complex, you need a map of your taste-buds to work it out. Brilliant.

FINISH Medium length but hangs together brilliantly. Still remains firm with the rye the dominant feature. Those gentle spices continue to buzz. Just like the rest of the whiskey the balance between sweet and dry is outstanding.

COMMENTS My favourite of all the Seagram whiskies and one of my top ten bourbons. It is absolutely overflowing with character. Enormous complexity that fills the mouth and makes the mouth water. It is hard to believe that Bourbon Street, a rather poor whiskey that was dragged unceremoniously off the market, came from the same stable.

PENNSYLVANIA WHISKEY

It seems almost unthinkable that there is no whiskey distillery operating in Pennsylvania today. Unthinkable, but true. Pennsylvania, along with Maryland and Kentucky was once one of *the* distilling centres. At the outbreak of World War II Pennsylvania was home to 42 whiskey distilleries. But in 1988, when the Michter Distillery in Schaefferstown closed its gates for the last time, a part of a nation's distilling heritage vanished almost without anyone noticing.

Ironically, as distilling had been carried out on the site since 1753 the ancient buildings have been designated a national landmark and are safe from the bulldozer. But that did not save the thousands of barrels of whiskey which had been maturing in the warehouses since its closure. Unguardable and of questionable quality, in 1996 the whiskey was destroyed by court order.

But there is some Pennsylvanian whiskey out there in the world's market place, and some of it is nothing short of stupendous. The trouble is, the label doesn't tell you where it is from: it is marked only as bourbon. But make a point of looking out for Hirsch 19- and 20-year-olds. They are owned, bottled and sold by the Hue family of Covington, Kentucky, who own the Cork 'n' Bottle liquor stores there. Originally, 1974 stocks of Michter whiskey were bought by a German called Adolph Hirsch. The 16-year-old is also quite a capture, and has been dumped into steel containers so it ages no longer. Sadly, though, there are only limited stocks available.

The whiskey was made with an exceptionally high rye content. But it is not rye whiskey. Although Michters was a Pennsylvanian distillery, in its later years it made only bourbon. That had not always been the case. When the Shenk family began distilling in the mid-18th century, it seems almost inconceivable that they did not distil rye at the old distillery and by the early 19th century the Shenks had moved into full commercial production of rye.

The distillery was silent between the start of Prohibition and the end of World War II. In the 1950s a new brand was launched: Michter's Pot Still bourbon. One of the Beam family had been brought over from Kentucky to get the distillery up and running and this he did, using a genuine pot still - legend has it shipped over from Scotland or Ireland - for the second distillation. The added copper in the distillation process may account for Hirsch 16-year-old's superbly rich texture. Whatever, on the evidence of this bottling, it is obvious the distillery should never have been allowed to die.

HIRSCH • 19-YEAR-OLD • 93 PROOF

Some extra oak has dulled the honeycomb but what an amazing whiskey for its age. Nothing like so complex as the 16-year-old but the way it packs a punch at such an old age borders on the unbelievable. Great stuff - one to be experienced. And it is fitting that the biggest contributor should be the rye, the very grain Pennsylvania became famous for.

HIRSCH RESERVE • 16-YEAR-OLD • 91.6 PROOF

NOSE Honeycomb and caramel engulf the nose while rye and wood-smoke hang around in the background. As it warms in the glass this does become quite complex with an unlikely addition of freshly cut cucumber and plums also joining the fun. Genuinely charming.

TASTE Seriously complex stuff which follows the complexity of the nose. The arrival on the palate is just brimming with soft corn and oak notes before a big honey sweetness follows through to form a slightly oily, excellent middle.

FINISH Honey, dried dates and rye are in full evidence but fall away as the age begins to gain revenge with some dry oak spoiling the party.

COMMENTS The finish may have slightly too much oak, but that is only a minor irritation. No bourbon spending this amount of time in the cask should be as good as this. Hugely enjoyable mainly thanks to those honey tones.

HIRSCH FINEST RESERVE • 20-YEAR-OLD
91.6 PROOF

NOSE The oakiness has kept in line with the 19-year-old, though the honeycomb has diminished further but is still there. Shades of liquorice now to keep the corn and rye company. Still very pleasing.

TASTE A very sure hand as it arrives on the palate with a subtle sweetness leading in the rye which has become slightly more prominent after a passing year and much more mouth-watering. The oak does arrive a shade earlier but if anything shows better restraint than its younger brother. Remarkably crisp and well defined for its age.

FINISH Some long oaky notes have an acceptable sappiness and the corn now makes it play. Some gentle caramel notes are playing as it finally drifts off.

COMMENTS Even better than the 19-year-old, this boasts greater balance and lucidity on the palate. Hardly any leather on this one and it is the small grains which must really stand up and take a bow. Brilliant. Now bring on the 21-year-old!

VIRGINIA WHISKEY

The bullet hole and shrapnel marks which scar the otherwise beautiful and elegant old buildings of Fredericksburg are the legacy of a nation at war. They could almost be symbolic of what has happened to the Virginian whiskey industry. A generation before the Civil War there was more whiskey made in Virginia than in Kentucky. A century and a half later and all that stands between Virginia whiskey going the same way as that of the Maryland and Pennsylvanian whiskey industries is a single copper pot still.

I have heard an argument that Virginian whiskey is alive, well and kicking in the Bluegrass state: after all, Kentucky was in 1792 carved from Virginia's Fincastle County. But it was not a very strong argument. And there are those who claim the last surviving Virginian whiskey, Virginia Gentleman, is not Virginian at all, but Kentucky. I don't agree with that either.

Certainly, a good number of Kentucky's earliest distillers did hail from Virginia. But the distilling operation in Fredericksburg today has always and proudly been an Old Dominion concern. What purists do have trouble coming to terms with is that the mashing, fermenting and first part of the distillation is actually carried out in Kentucky. It is the spirit which is shipped to Fredericksburg where the old copper pot turns what was originally bourbon designate into Virginia designate.

This has only recently been the case. In 1935 A. Smith Bowman built the distillery in the rolling pastures of Renton a few miles south of the Potomac river. It was a welcome injection into a state that had seen its industry whittled down to just five distilleries shortly before Prohibition. Now Washington DC and Alexandria have stretched right out to meet it and on the other side of town is Washington's Dulles Airport. The company's present president, Jay Adams, a relative of Bowman by marriage, decided to shut up shop and move south when it became no longer viable for the whole distilling process to be carried out in Virginia. He relocated in a former cellophane factory which gives all the appearances of a post-Prohibition distillery. And every now and then the old pot still is swung into action to turn the spirit, originally made with Renton's original 20 per cent rye recipe at the now lost Heaven Hill plant, into the next batch of Virginia Gentleman.

Until 1996 there were still a few barrels of Renton whiskey. It can still be spotted now and again at the back of liquor stores: if you find a Virginia Gentleman with a slightly plainer label than the others and it is called Virginia whiskey as opposed to Virginia bourbon, then congratulations! You have found yourself a genuine, all-time classic American whiskey. The new bottlings are delightfully drinkable but just don't have the same weight and beguiling small grain complexity offered by the old Virginia. whiskey, which was unquestionably one of the best bourbons it has been my privilege to discover.

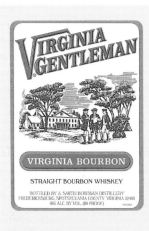

VIRGINIA BOURBON

STRAIGHT BOURBON WHISKEY

BOTTLED BY A. SMITH BOWMAN DISTILLERY
FREDERICKSBURG, SPOTSYLVANIA COUNTY, VIRGINIA 22408
40% ALC. BY VOL. (80 PROOF)

VIRGINIA GENTLEMAN VIRGINIA BOURBON 80 PROOF

NOSE Very light and bares no comparison to the original Virginia Gentleman save a hint of honey which carries well on the malt. Very attractive.

TASTE Heavier than you might expect from a bourbon that's been thrice through the distilling process. Lots of character with the first subtle signs of oak showing through quite early and playful, spicy grain following on behind.

FINISH Only on the finish does extra complexity show through. It is beautifully striated with traces of malt and rye hanging on with the vanilla from the oak blending in delightfully. Sometimes the malt is so powering, it is reminiscent of a single malt Scotch. Again, hints of spices dart about. This is the highlight of the bourbon.

COMMENTS When Jay Adams launched his new bourbon on the market he expected to be buried under an avalanche of phone calls from regular Virginia Gentleman drinkers wondering what in darnation had happened to their drink. The calls didn't come. This whiskey may have originated at Heaven Hill in Kentucky, but one pass through the old-fangled copper still at Fredericksburg, Virginia, and it has changed character completely and gained its own identity. Lighter in colour and character it may be, but Virginia Gentleman remains a hugely enjoyable, high-class whiskey.

VIRGINIA GENTLEMAN VIRGINIA WHISKEY 80 PROOF

NOSE Majestic mixture of perfect oak balance and complex sweet malts and maybe sandalwood and fine leather. There is acacia honey topped with soft spices. It is, frankly, one of the most delicate and beautiful noses it has ever been my pleasure to discover.

TASTE The delicacy is a perfect match on the palate. Oak is the very first to show, which did not used to be the case with Virginia Gentleman. But the dryness it carries is a superb foil to the ultra-intense malt.

FINISH The finish, perhaps thanks to the oak, is not quite as long or sweet as was the case a couple of years back. But dark chocolate has arrived to give the whiskey a silky, pleasantly crisp finish.

COMMENTS This is some whiskey, though the signs of age were beginning to show on the palate. The fact that it will never be seen again is nothing less than heartbreaking. I shall cherish my two remaining litres as if they were liquid gold.

TENNESSEE WHISKEY

"What is the difference between bourbon and Tennessee whiskey?" If I had a dollar for each time I was asked that question, my second car would be a Merc. Most people think that it is because Jack Daniel makes a big thing about sour mash. In fact all bourbon is sour mash, too. Others believe that it is because to be a bourbon you have to be made in Kentucky. Not true, either. Bourbon can be made anywhere in the United States - even Tennessee. And to say there is a particular Tennessee style would also be inaccurate. The two distilleries George Dickel and Jack Daniel make two very different whiskies, one moderately light and delicate the other heavy and bruising: they have about as much in common as peaty Islay malt and a gentle Speysider. They can't even agree which way it should be spelt: Daniel prefers whiskey while Dickel insists on whisky.

The actual difference between bourbon and Tennessee has to do with charcoal. With the possible exception of Maker's Mark just about every American whiskey undergoes a form of carbon filtration. But what is so different in Tennessee is that after the spirit has run from the still it undergoes a long filtering process in which it runs through about twelve feet of charcoal held in leaching vats, a four-day plus journey that ends with the cleansed spirit being barreled.

That is why, if you visit the Jack Daniel or George Dickel distilleries you might see a whole stack of maple wood going up in smoke in specially constructed ricks consisting of planks criss-crossing each other in layers. Like most things in whiskey, there is even a special art form to this, with the ricks leaning towards each other in the middle so they collapse inwardly as they burn. Local maple is the preferred choice for the planks as it is believed to add, even in charred form, a very delicate sweetness. This filtration process, the Lincoln County Process, is better known as charcoal mellowing, because some of the larger flavour-carrying congeners in the spirit are trapped as it trickles down through the carbon and finally out through a blanket of white wool.

Opposite
Maple wood is burnt in ricks to make charcoal for the filtration process which makes Tennessee whiskey unique.

In 1941 the American government belatedly recognized this peculiar activity and granted Tennessee a status by law equal to and distinct from bourbon and rye. Sadly by then there were only two distilleries to celebrate the fact, and one of those was making its whiskey in Kentucky. Prohibition had hit the God-fearing lands of Tennessee before most, arriving as early as 1910. Just over a century ago there were no fewer than 700 distilleries making legal whiskey, or bourbon as it was still regarded in those days. By 1913, three years into the ban, there were just seven - though none in production. And when Dickel returned to its home state in 1958 there remained, quite remarkably, only the one: Jack Daniel's.

JACK DANIEL

It is hard to argue against the claim that Jack Daniel's is the most famous whiskey in the world. The town where it is situated, Lynchburg, Tennessee, is very much like any other American mid-western or southern small town, except maybe that the downtown shops are prettier than most. The people are friendly, life has its own pace and when the summer months are at their hottest and humidity jumps off the charts, it gets slower still.

And for the best part of a century Jack Daniel's whiskey was most like any other. Until 1941 it was a bourbon, one that on occasion like thousands of others before and after came close to going out of business. Today, though, sales of Jack Daniel are such that the distillery's founder Jasper Newton Daniel, or Jack as he was known throughout his life, would have to pinch himself to believe.

The success of JD has confounded just about every market trend there has been. Sales of dark spirits have been on the wane: listen to any marketing guy and he will depress you with tales of how people prefer to drink something that tastes of nothing. Well, JD trumps that on both counts. Firstly, five or six Tennessee summers make for a very dark spirit. And second, Jack is

nothing if not brimming over with massive flavour - it is almost phenolic in its oily attack on the taste-buds. And while it is extremely popular as a mixer, especially with coke, both the young and the not so young seem to enjoy banging it down neat.

For me, likewise, there are times when I must get my hands on a glass, usually late at night when I'm quite tired after a long drive. It is enormous whiskey and its finish hangs around the palate for a long time, sticking deliciously to the roof of the mouth. In its straightforward, world renowned Black Label variety, don't look for subtlety. And as for complexity, forget it. It is a restorative supreme. And I can tell you without any fear of error: there is no other whiskey in the

world which has so much oil and muscle in its delivery.

There is a very simple reason for this. In effect, Jack Daniel's is distilled just the once. Beneath the four enormous beer stills which serve the battery of fermenters there is a doubler. But all that services is the vapour off the beer heater. So Jack Daniel's spirit is about as oily and uncompromising as a spirit gets. But if you try the new generation of small batch older whiskies, which have matured a few extra years, it is quite surprising just how much of this fatness is subdued by the oak. Even so, it never tastes like anything other than JD.

Young Jack Daniel began his distillery in 1866, having learnt his trade during the Civil War. The spot he chose for his enterprise was beside a perfect source for the water he required, Cave Spring. Each year now hundreds of thousands of people come to visit that sight, as the Daniels Distillery is still there today. But it had not always

Right
A Jack Daniel's
maturing
barrelhouse.

been. In 1909, Moore County, in which Lynchburg is situated, became dry. One year later so, too, did the entire State. Jack never married, so the distillery was run by nephew Lem Motlow who simply decided to move states, and until the entire country was gripped by Prohibition the Daniel distillery operated out of St Louis, Missouri, a city, with all its breweries, also blessed for its waters.

Jack lived just long enough to see his beloved distillery move home. He died in 1911 from the very long and agonising complications resulting from a broken toe. It happened when in a fit of temper he kicked his safe after being unable to open it.

Motlow was further frustrated by Tennessee's refusal to end Prohibition when the blanket ban on drinking was revoked. Finally in 1938 Tennessee had a change of heart and allowed their now most famous product to come home. For the last 30 years Jack Daniel's has been in the hands of another family-run company, Brown-Foreman, under whom the brand has flourished.

Throughout his life Daniel had battled ceaselessly to get his brand noticed, entering it in as many competitions he could and taking pride in the medals it won. He yearned for international recognition and now he has it beyond his wildest dreams. Some look at JD's success coldly as a simple case of successful marketing. I look at it with more than a degree of romance. But, then, seeing how his English grandfather only came to America in order to elope with his 15-year-old Scottish bride, what do you expect?

Below
Uncle Jack's –
another long
gone Daniel's
brand.

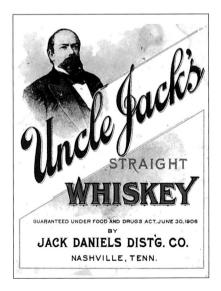

GENTLEMAN JACK • 80 PROOF

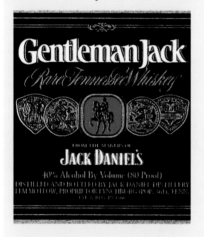

For some reason the marketing guys make a point of boasting that Gentleman Jack is "The first new whiskey to be introduced by our distillery for more than a century". So what were Jack Daniel's Black Label (1911) and Lem Motlow's (1939)? As I always say: take whatever is written on the labels with a pinch of malt.

What is beyond dispute is the truly unique method of filtration which sets Gentleman Jack apart from any other Tennessee whiskey. At both Daniel and Dickel, the spirit which runs from the stills is charcoal mellowed before being filled into the barrel. To create Gentleman Jack, the blenders came up with the novel idea of choosing a 4-year-old whiskey fit enough for Green Label and then, before, bottling, running it through the charcoal filter for a second time. The result is an extraordinarily low-key whiskey but one without a single hint of blandness. It is sold throughout the 50 US States but has as yet to find an export market.

JACK DANIEL

NOSE A real softy. All aspects of the aroma are gentle and quietly persuasive. It is still, however, unmistakably Jack Daniel's thanks to that unique burnt-something-or-other aroma.

TASTE Smooth and oily to begin and seems to mould itself to the contours of the mouth. Starts faintly dry and then sweetens with tell-tale liquorice-burnt molasses feel arriving but never gripping with the drum-thumping authority of the ordinary Jack.

FINISH A real low-level finale. Lots of sweet liquorice, but at one point there is even a rich cocoa character which gives way to the burnt treacle.

COMMENTS A refined whiskey with virtually none of the gung-ho attributed to ordinary Jack yet retaining a distinct Jack Daniel's character. Out and out JD devotees will often tell you they find this TOO smooth!

JACK DANIEL'S BARREL HOUSE 1 • 94 PROOF

This whiskey was hand selected to commemorate one of the oldest operating barrelhouses at the Jack Daniel Distillery, Barrelhouse 1, tract 1.
Bottled at __94__ proof, from batch No. __B-00__ in the summer of 1994.

DISTILLED AND BOTTLED BY JACK DANIEL DISTILLERY LEM MOTLOW, PROPRIETOR, LYNCHBURG (POP. 361), TENN.
TENNESSEE WHISKEY • 750ML
ALCOHOL 47% BY VOLUME (94 PROOF)
GOVERNMENT WARNING: (1) ACCORDING TO THE SURGEON GENERAL, WOMEN SHOULD NOT DRINK ALCOHOLIC BEVERAGES DURING PREGNANCY BECAUSE OF THE RISK OF BIRTH DEFECTS. (2) CONSUMPTION OF ALCOHOLIC BEVERAGES IMPAIRS YOUR ABILITY TO DRIVE A CAR OR OPERATE MACHINERY, AND MAY CAUSE HEALTH PROBLEMS.

On 1 January 1995 a brand-new whiskey was launched by Jack Daniel's to mark the opening of their on-site liquor store. At 2.55p.m. on 29 April 29 1995 the store closed: they had sold out. Such was the impact of this wonderful whisky, the first in years Jack Daniel's used a cork stopper for. During 1994 both Tennessee distilleries had been given the go-ahead to sell whiskey direct from the distillery for the first time since 1916. One of the original prerequisites was that the whiskey on sale had to be different from any other marketed by the company. This gave master blender Lincoln Henderson the chance he had long been looking for to develop for a ready-made market a Jack Daniel of a quality few thought possible. Lincoln had for many years known that the very finest barrels came from the "Buzzards Roost" of Number 1 warehouse - Barrel House 1.

The "Buzzard's Roost" was the very top layer of barrels closest to the roof of the iron-clad warehouse. I have tasted samples from barrels as they matured in that rarefied atmosphere - their delicious intensity is phenomenal, quite different from anything else I have experienced. Only 500 barrels can be kept there at any one time. To keep the small batch whiskey going the distillers have now undertaken a programme of moving 5-year-old barrels into the roost to spend exactly a year in the top flight cooker before bottling. Previously, they may have been on the top floor of the south warehouses or floors five or six of Barrel House 1. Because of the exclusivity of the small-batch whiskey the name Barrel House 1 was given to the new brand. It could have been "Route 66" - there are

66 steps from the ground to the Buzzard's Roost. But, as I discovered, it is well worth the journey.

NOSE
Mightily intense with heaps of oak. For best results allow to sit in the glass and oxidize for a few minutes and it will take on a superbly balanced grassy character unique to this amongst all the Jack Daniel's brands. Enticingly sweet throughout.

TASTE A big whiskey with a glorious, malty start. The sweetness pervades from the first taste to the expansive middle where the oak takes hold yet retains the richness of a fine dark Guyanan pot still rum.

FINISH Very long, very slow to develop. The maltiness has been replaced by echoes of spicy rye alongside a tangy woodiness. Quite superb.

COMMENTS This is a classic whiskey by any standards, quite simply the best thing from the distillery. If you do visit, make sure to take a bottle back, as this, though retaining the unmistakable Jack Daniels DNA, is a relative far removed. Like the Master Distiller, it enjoys a healthy degree of complexity but this is easily the pick of the crop and a sheer delight to the taste-buds.

JACK DANIEL'S GREEN LABEL • 80 PROOF

This is the original Jack Daniel's. Launched in 1884, the distinctive green label was synonymous with this Tennessee whiskey until the launch of Black Label nearly 35 years later. Like all Jack Daniel's whiskey, it is made to the mashbill of 80 per cent corn, 12 per cent rye and 8 per cent malted barley. What sets it apart from all but one other Jack Daniel's brands, is its youth: it is a 4-year-old. However, there was until recently a much younger whiskey from Jack Daniel's launched in 1939, a year after the new building of the distillery and called after the proprietor, Lem Motlow. That whiskey was just a year old when bottled and was brought on to the market to bring in some quick cash. Originally sold nationally, its market dwindled to just Tennessee and Georgia where some regarded it the finest brand of all. LEM MOTLOW'S TENNESSEE WHISKEY, with its strangely proud boast: "This whiskey is 12 months old" was last bottled in 1992. It had a ferocious pear-drop nose but had already matured into a whiskey similar to a 4-year-old Islay malt full of smoky phenols but gazelle-like as it darted around the palate. The off-balance finish was thin in character to say the least, yet surprisingly oaky. Overall, Lem Motlow's was a taste of things to come. The fuller, oilier Green Label cannot be found outside North America and apart from small pockets around Virginia, Washington DC and New Mexico is now sold only in the south-eastern quarter of the USA.

JACK DANIEL

NOSE The lightest of all Jack Daniel's. There is a nip and bite to the nose which give away its tender years, although the heavy oiliness is nothing like as profound as its famous Black Label brother. Lurking somewhere beyond this astringency is a hint of apple and corn.

TASTE A dry, bracing start where the distinctive Jack Daniel's burnt liquorice character clatters into the taste-buds without the oily buffer unique to its famous older relation. The middle proves softer, sweeter and milder and not devoid of a certain unpretentious charm.

FINISH Dries again for the finale. It is a long finish, unusually long for a whiskey of this age and this has to be because of the oils which cling to the roof of the mouth. The very last notes are those, once again, of dry liquorice. Despite this, the overall feel is of a cleaner, crisper whiskey than one associates with the Daniel's name.

COMMENTS A bit of a shock when first tasted, Green Label offers little sophistication but does grow on you. In its favour is a remarkable ability to make the taste-buds continuously second-guess what is going to happen next. Quite a character and one markedly different from Lem Motlow.

JACK DANIEL'S OLD NO. 7 BRAND • 86 PROOF

So powerful is the Jack Daniel name, that few today are aware that the whiskey they drink from that famous square bottle is called the Old No. 7 Brand. Instead, people will ask for a "Jack", a "JD" or a Jack Daniel's. The No. 7 name was born, it is claimed, thanks to a visit Jack Daniel made to a friend in near by Tullahoma. His friend owned a string of stores, seven in all. With Daniel not quite happy with the original "Belle of Lincoln" epithet, he grabbed at the number 7 and turned it into a brand name. That, I'm afraid, is the uninspiring story behind it, although there was another tale spun, apparently by Lem Motlow. His theory was that seven barrels went missing and when they were found a clerk marked them as number 7. People who re-ordered the whiskey then asked for more of the "Number 7" brand.

What is not in dispute is why a new black label whiskey was sold alongside the Green Label. When Jack Daniel died in 1911 Lem Motlow brought out an older-aged whiskey in honour of Jack complete with a black label as mark of respect. To set the two whiskies apart, the Black Label contained older, more fully matured whiskey, which is still the case today. Where the Green Label was a 4-year-old, Black Label is a mixture of 5- and 6-year-olds, but like the Green Label comprises a balanced mixture of barrels from all four floors of the south warehouse complex. But what a difference that extra year or two makes! Originally marketed locally, sales developed nationally after Prohibition and it is today the biggest-selling American whiskey the world over.

NOSE Assertive and uncompromising, this a truly unique nose amongst North American whiskies. Phenolic and fiery in character, its backbone is the massive liquorice which has linked with the oak to produce a heavy and sweet aroma.

TASTE Boom! Although the sledge-hammer start momentarily shatters the senses, you are aware of a clinging oiliness which soon smoothes things down. This makes for a surprisingly gentle middle...gentle, that is, if you can handle a mouthful of singed liquorice and cremated treacle toffee.

FINISH Enormously long, almost never-ending. Becomes increasingly dry but for a few, fleeting seconds you can at last pick out a subtle corn-malt complexity. When that has passed it's back to the oak, oil and charred remains, although the very final notes sweeten up delightfully.

COMMENTS Some whiskey, this. And very much an acquired taste. It holds a cult status around the world while many other bourbon-Tennessee connoisseurs cannot stand the stuff. But it is probably those who, like myself, enjoy heavy, peaty malt whiskies from Islay who eventually see the beauty in the beast. To drink straight is not for the faint-hearted and although it lacks finesse there is such fun and good nature amid the brute force that familiarity breeds anything but contempt.

JACK DANIEL SILVER SELECT SINGLE BARREL 100 PROOF

The most powerful JD on the market and available from Duty Free only. Despite its strength it is lighter in body than other JD special editions and outwardly youngish on the palate. Stunning bitter-sweet battle for supremacy with deep vanillas ensuring a dry, chalky finish with a big bitter chocolate finale. Although quintessential JD, this one does have an individualistic style.

JACK DANIEL'S SINGLE BARREL • 94 PROOF (90 PROOF EXPORT)

NOSE No mistaking another Jack Daniel here. Not as intense an aroma as Barrel House 1; thinner with perhaps one or two blemishes coming through with those uncompromising phenols just being slightly out of sync' Yet having said that, for Daniel's devotees still a typically enticing and sweet nose with some solid oak providing the buttress.

TASTE Initially soft and melt-in-the-mouth. Only after a few seconds does the oiliness filter through with the burnt-liquorice effect. The highlight is the excellent middle with fine malt and rye character.

FINISH Somewhat thinner and maltier than you might expect with soft oakiness leading the fade-ut. But there is a deft peppery spiciness which hangs around thanks mainly to confident rye and malt.

COMMENTS Delicious stuff but rather strange for a JD. It never really lets rip like the great Jacks do, is not as oily as the distillery's mould dictates yet has sufficient weight and richness to put it firmly into the Jack Daniel style. The combined malt and rye small grains have a bigger say here than probably any other JD brand. As can be the case with single barrels, can be less than perfect but intriguing and hugely enjoyable none the less.

MASTER DISTILLER • 90 PROOF

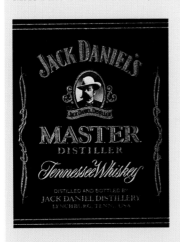

When Master Distiller was launched on 16 September 1993, it became the first whiskey from the distillery to be sold exclusively abroad. What was more, its sole market was Japan where it was introduced to fight head-on with 12-year-old bourbons from IW Harper and Wild Turkey and the Single Barrels of Blanton's and Bookers. The thousand barrels chosen to be vatted were 6 years old, all taken from the fourth floor - the very top - of the distillery's south warehouses. To try this whiskey you must travel to Japan and then part with around 8,000 yen.

NOSE Rich and sweet like whiskey truffles. Somehow deeper than ordinary Jack with greater emphasis on the oak.

TASTE Fills the mouth with a resounding corn-oak dominance. The middle sweetens a little with a sappy-liquorice thrust.

FINISH Very long and extremely elegant. The first notes, surprisingly, are some rye-shaped hardness followed by a dry oakiness and then backed up again by the rye. Late coffee/cocoa notes develop but it is all very low key.

COMMENTS By far the best Jack Daniel's sold away from the distillery. Certainly, it is the only one where the grains dominate at the cost of the heavy oil that are a trade-mark of all the other brands. With the corn and rye having such a big say in the character of the whiskey this one deserves recognition amongst the top bourbon-styles, even though its full character, so appreciated by the Japanese, may still be a hard hurdle to clear for some bourbon devotees.

GEORGE DICKEL

People who talk about Tennessee having a distinctive style should spend a quiet half an hour with a glass of George Dickel No. 12. Once it was a bourbon and in character it still is. Strike lucky and the bottle you buy may be even better than a ten-year-old Ancient Age, and that is no mean achievement.

If any two distilleries in North America do have a similarity in nose and taste (let's forget about the two Jim Beam plants) then Ancient Age and Dickel are they. This is, of course, sheer fluke. When Dickel returned to Tennessee in 1958 after a near half century's exile, there was no knowing just what the local water, bought-in grains and shape of the stills were going to conjure together. But there may have been a small clue: George Dickel works to a high corn recipe of 81/11/8, which is only a percentage point here and there away from AA's similarly high-corn formula.

And as fate would have it, Dickel once distilled at Frankfort (see Ancient Age). But really, in the way that fate seems to insist on completing winding circuits throughout the history of American distilling, Dickel was destined to spend some time in Kentucky's capital, because

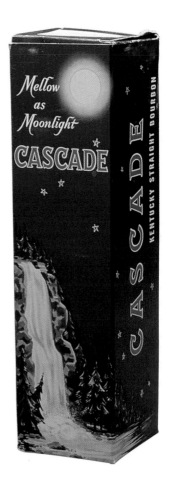

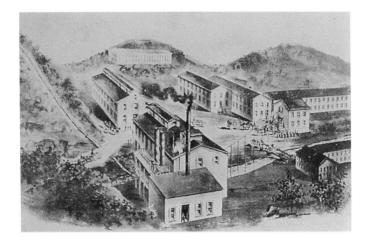

the George Dickel who gave his name to the distillery was a German originally from Frankfurt am Main. He is believed to have landed in America while still in his mid-twenties but it was not until he was in his sixties that he went into distilling for the first time, although he was in the whiskey wholesale trade for a decade before he took the plunge. The site he chose was a remote spot a few miles along winding country lanes from the railroad town of Tullahoma. This little haven is called Cascade Hollow and even today, a few hundred yards from the new distillery, you can clearly define the stone outlines of Dickel's first, simple enterprise.

It has been left to nature since 1910 when Tennessee went dry. The company moved to the Stitzel Weller distillery in Louisville until 1937

Above
The Cascade distillery at the turn of the century.
Opposite
Cascade packaging – the bottle is from the 30s and the presentation box is from the 50s.

when Dickel became part of the Schenley empire and production was moved to Ancient Age.

No trip to Tennessee is complete without popping into Dickel's. The plant from the outside is softer than most architectural creations of the late 1950s, but its brick still jars a little with the unremitting pastoral beauty which surrounds it. The Cascade Creek runs by the distillery and on the other side is a glorious log cabin which acts as distillery shop but equally throws you back to an age when the original old stone distillery was in operation. Also at the distillery can be seen a 100-year-old bottle of

Below
The driveway up to the Cascade distillery today.

Dickel's original Cascade Hollow brand. Daringly he called it Tennessee Whisky (without the 'e', a tradition that has been kept) when many others, Jack Daniel included, were calling theirs bourbon.

The inside of the distillery is much like any other, rather more spotless, perhaps and the doubler is curious for being stainless steel but heated by copper tubes. Another interesting point is the charcoal mellowing method employed by Dickel. Where Jack Daniel have just a single woollen blanket at the bottom of their charcoal, Dickel also have one at the top. This is to try to ensure that the spirit seeps from the top into as wide an area of the charcoal as possible and not drip down into one spot.

There have been one or two new Dickel brands of late. There has been a ten-year-old doing the rounds in Europe and one called RX, which is actually distilled at Stitzel Weller. Neither, though, holds a candle to the magnificent and still under-appreciated No. 12 brand. That is an eight-year-old of finesse that most distillers can only dream about. Every distillery has its optimum age. This is it for Dickel, and no amount of extra ageing will ever change that fact.

GEORGE DICKEL OLD NO. 8 BRAND • 80 PROOF

The nose does little to get you to drink this one. Yet I love the youthful, fizzing attack as it crash-lands on to the tastebuds. A whisky which grows on you.

GEORGE DICKEL SPECIAL BARREL RESERVE 10-YEAR-OLD • 86 PROOF

NOSE The rye comes out screaming on this one. The extra age in the wood has ensured a spiciness which has a significant say. There are more noticeable floral notes, as well. A lot more intense than the trusty No. 12 brand, though perhaps not quite so tantalizing.

TASTE A silky, oily start of astounding beauty. There is enormous sweetness, slightly sappy in texture and mouth-feel as the oak comes in early. But there is a big toffee middle that is flatter and a lot smoother than other Dickels.

FINISH The toffee continues in a very big way and manages to keep out any drying oak. Slightly creamy at the end. Very, very long.

COMMENTS A whisky of major significance. Nothing like so complex as the No. 12 brand, but still an almighty whisky with great character.

GEORGE DICKEL SUPERIOR NO. 12 BRAND
90 PROOF

NOSE Don't bother nosing when cold. Let this warm up on the hand and you will put Tennessee whisky into another world. There are fresh leather, sweetcorn, butter, butterscotch, apples and so much more. But none stands out: there are just teasing hints of each. Aaah!

TASTE Absolutely stunning start. A kaleidoscope of tastes swamps the taste-buds and you are left reeling. I'm not sure any other North American whisky starts off with such elegance, class and complexity. There is just a touch of acacia honey to sweeten things up while the more labyrinthine notes take command. Oily rye and vanilla are amongst them.

The trick is to go with the flow and just ride those flavour waves crashing against the taste-buds…whatever they are carrying.

FINISH Just gentle strains of toffee and vanilla is all there is to show in the dying embers.

COMMENTS A world classic. Yet one of the hardest whiskies in the world to describe because the flavour profile changes so often on the palate your brain never gets more than a nano-second to work out just what it is focusing in on. Just when you think you are getting close, it is gone! A whisky I suggest everyone should try to see exactly what I mean.

Above
The Dickel distillery store, for all your liquid supplies.

RYE WHISKEY

If any whiskey style in the world more needs, or is more deserving, of a revival than straight rye then I have yet to find it. Rye was for a long time a staple of the American drinker. As we have seen from the history of whiskey-making in America, George Washington was himself a rye distiller and until bourbon became firmly established, rye was the dominant whiskey type in America. Even as late as the 1940s, Mount Vernon rye from Maryland and Old Overholt from Pennsylvania were major brands.

But the decline in demand for rye whiskey since World War II has already seen the extinction of the industries of Pennsylvania and Maryland. It is unlikely to hit Kentucky but there are only three distillers marketing it, Jim Beam, Wild Turkey and Heaven Hill, while in California the Anchor Distillery has made a singular rye malt whiskey. An astonishing rye whiskey is produced in Indiana but that is destined only for blends.

It was a change in a nation's taste that brought about the untimely death of so many great rye distilleries. Before Prohibition distillers were so proud of what they made they even incorporated it into their names: the Philadelphia Pure Rye Distilling Company of Eddington, PA; the Mountain Spring Pure Rye Distilling Company of Burkittsville, Maryland; the Maryland Pure Rye Distillery Company of Baltimore - just three of 65 distilleries in Maryland and Pennsylvania. But the banning of legal drinking in America saw people buying what they could get, and that usually meant a very light-flavoured spirit, indeed. Rye is many things, but it is not light. Indeed, only the peaty Islay malt whiskies of Scotland compete with it as the most flavoursome whiskey style found on earth.

And that, perhaps, is why I am determined to see rye's comeback. To be rye, it has to be made from a minimum 51 per cent rye, just as bourbon has to be made from 51 per cent corn. And it also has to be matured in virgin oak barrels. Rye being a sharp, fruity grain when mashed produces a distilled spirit that is enormously complex and challenging on the palate, richly textured and deep in flavour and finish. It is the kind of whiskey that connoisseurs the world over are trying to find, but in most cases don't even know that it still exists. Trying to find rye outside America or Japan is often a pointless exercise.

Rye has been caught in a vicious circle. Because so little of it is made - Wild Turkey, for instance, makes a rye mash just once a year - the marketing people are loath to spend any money pushing it. Even if there is a demand for it, there is insufficient stock to keep any momentum going. So for the last 20 years brands have been serving old loyalists, sad to say many of whom are dying out. Even a plan by United Distillers to market a beautiful fifteen-year-old effort from the now defunct Buffalo Distillery and a slightly less charming sixteen-year-old from Stagg (Ancient Age) Distillery has been shelved due to their merger with IDV.

The brilliant news is that in the Spring of 1998 Ancient Age decided to make rye once more, using the same 51 percent rye recipe from the Stagg days. This first rye to be produced at the great Frankfort distillery for a decade and a half will be marketed as a four-year-old in 2002.

So there is hope. And at least one entrepreneurial type has begun selling some old stocks found in distilleries not normally known for their rye. And you can rest assured that I'm doing all I can to get a brand going in Europe and around the world to help heighten interest in what I regard as probably my favourite whiskey style of all.

JIM BEAM RYE • 80 PROOF

NOSE One of the most magical noses in the world with the rye zipping through from the off with mint and perhaps a hint of lavender in there for good measure. A sweet, rich, spicy and vaguely oily nose. The most aromatic commercial rye whiskey made today.

THE WORLD'S FINEST RYE

JIM BEAM RYE

40% ALC/VOL   (80 PROOF)

STRAIGHT RYE WHISKEY

NONE GENUINE WITHOUT MY SIGNATURE

DISTILLED AND BOTTLED BY

JAMES B. BEAM DISTILLING CO.
BEAM • CLERMONT
FRANKFORT, KENTUCKY USA

TASTE Wow! An astonishing bombardment on the taste-buds from the very start. The rye oil takes first grip then the grain itself follows through with a superb, mouthwatering explosion of juicy, ripe plumy fruit and a rigid hardness.

FINISH Really long and flinty hard with late oaky-chocolate notes to round things off to near perfection.

COMMENTS It is beyond my comprehension that a whiskey, indeed any beverage, of this quality can be near impossible to find. This a rye that grabs the taste-buds and refuses to let go. Absolutely superb.

OLD OVERHOLT

80 PROOF

FROM JIM BEAM

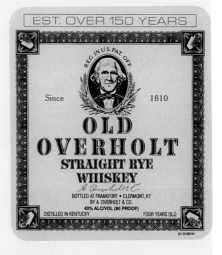

NOSE Creamier, milkier, less rye and spice infested. Some citrus notes also lighten the rye out by comparison with stablemate Jim Beam.

TASTE Fatter and creamier textured at first with the rye holding back its full force for the first few waves. Although evident from the first few seconds, it arrives powerfully but chalky dry. A rock solid rye texture forms the middle.

FINISH A significantly drier finish with a similar cocoa-rye pattern to the Jim Beam but nothing like so sweet or fruity.

COMMENTS This is quite a different proposition from the Jim Beam rye; not quite so full-frontal and flashy in its rye character at first but with a delightful subtlety once the rye arrives. This is the sort of whiskey which grows slowly on you until you are ultimately seduced by its wily charms.

PIKESVILLE • 80 PROOF • FROM HEAVEN HILL

REGISTERED U.S. PATENT OFFICE

PIKESVILLE

TRADE — *STRAIGHT RYE WHISKEY* — MARK

SUPREME

STRAIGHT RYE WHISKEY

40% ALC/VOL (80 PROOF)

BOTTLED BY
Standard Distillers Products Company
BARDSTOWN, KENTUCKY 40004

NOSE Something strangely akin to the odour of the inside of a brand new car. Leathery, sweet, slightly spiced. Oh, yes. There is rye in there, as well.

TASTE Velvet soft but the rye hits early and hits hard. There is a sweet mintiness that softens the rigidity of the rye that dominates the middle.

FINISH Long and chewy. The only commercial rye where caramel features to any degree but this is blown away by a build-up first of vanilla and then rye. The dry oakiness hangs around for some time.

COMMENTS Extremely busy rye hits home very hard throughout this wonderful dram. Not quite as complex as the Beams and Wild Turkeys of the rye world but a hell of a drink none the less. Very enjoyable.

RITTENHOUSE RYE • 80 PROOF • FROM HEAVEN HILL

Whisky spelt without an "e"! Made for the Pennsylvanian market, this was formerly produced by Medley.

NOSE You could have your head over a steaming mash of rye: it is sweet, doughy with hints of cinnamon, lemon and stewed cherries. Really sexy. And quite light, too.

TASTE Beautifully balanced, fat and sweet and then a big fruity rye punch surges through the middle. The rye hits home in a big way, but then the punches are soft and controlled. A thin layer of demerara sweetens things a little

FINISH Amazingly dark, moody and sweet. Lingering smokiness and ripe plums and roasted almonds. Only at the very end does the rye rumble through with something approaching brittleness by which time some peppery spices warm things up a little.

COMMENTS Quite superb. Does change slightly from bottling to bottling in intensity. But this is as soft as candyfloss, the gentlest rye I have ever encountered. A classic to keep at home if you can find it.

STEPHEN FOSTER • 80 PROOF • FROM HEAVEN HILL

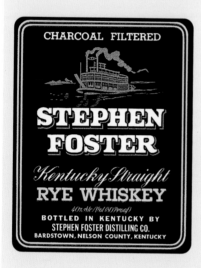

NOSE Just a little feinty; rather young with the soft grains offering spicy complexity but little intensity.

TASTE Unbelievably soft. The silky oiliness has gentle, fruity rye flavours and an accompanying fatness. But limited depth or scope.

FINISH Rye has detached itself from all else and furrows a lone path. Quite hard and angular but lacking balance.

COMMENTS A disappointing rye that is meant to be the same as Pikesville and Rittenhouse but is obviously lacking. Not particularly well made.

OLD RIP VAN WINKLE'S OLD TIME RYE
12-YEAR-OLD • 90 PROOF

VAN WINKLE'S FAMILY RESERVE RYE
13-YEAR-OLD • 95.6 PROOF

These two, for all intents and purposes, are exactly the same whiskey. The barrels are currently housed in a warehouse at the Old Hoffman Distillery which stands by the Salt river in one of the most scenic parts of Anderson County where the road heads for some gentle hills. The distillery is near Lawrenceburg, Ky, and not surprisingly once part of the ancient Ripy distilling empire. But the whiskey comes from somewhere else entirely: the Medley Distillery at Owensboro, about as far west as the Kentucky whiskey industry ever ventured.

A century ago the whiskies of Daviess county were famed, but it was a rye produced by Monarch which had most respect of all. The late Medley Distillery, silent since being owned by Glenmore, originally made this whiskey for their old Rittenhouse brand which eventually went to Heaven Hill via Glenmore Distillers, and was unearthed by Julian Van Winkle, president of the Old Rip Van Winkle Company in response to demands for rye from the Japanese market. The result is this 12-13-year-old which was bottled at his silent

253

Hoffman Distillery just a week or two before Christmas 1997. The rye is already available in Kentucky, making it the oldest rye being sold in the state almost in living memory and he hopes the rye will not only hit the Japanese market, but Europe's as well.

NOSE Soft oak and a bourbony, vanilla sweetness slightly overpower the harder rye tones. There is also a distinctly perfumed note, almost soapy. An intriguing and very different aroma from any whiskey I have ever nosed. At a lower strength both malt and corn are noticeable and the small grains work in delightful harmony.

TASTE Again the oak is fast off the blocks and holds the palate's attention for the first seven or eight seconds before the rye starts to thunder through. Although it makes it to the front, it is quickly caught up and then overtaken again by the oak. An excellent rye oiliness and rich mouth-feel continue. Very little of the fruitiness one expects from a Kentucky rye, but there is also something vaguely liquour-ish

FINISH Extremely dry with a minty coolness and some cocoa notes again associated with the oak. Medium length, chalky and some corn follow-through. The rye does make a bitter-sweet fruity entrance just before the close.

COMMENTS A very unusual rye, not exactly a standard bearer for its genre. Having said that it remains a wonderful mouth filler, and a whiskey quite unlike the many thousands I have tasted before. This is not a whiskey to be sipped. For best results take a very large mouthful and keep on the palate for a good 20 seconds. Once you get past the oak, the ride is an enjoyable one. Although identical whiskies, the 13-year-old is better to taste, yet the 12 wins on the nose.

WILD TURKEY
101 PROOF

NOSE Even in its straight rye the honeyed Wild Turkey trademark is there in force from the very first sniff. So too is the rye grain but much less forceful than its colleagues at Beam and Heaven Hill.

TASTE Rye is the first, second and third thing to swamp the palate from the very start. There is a honey-wax sweetness and richness which acts as the most seductive counterbalance you can imagine.

FINISH Beautifully long with some stem ginger, soft corn and vanilla dovetailing with the rye. Classic stuff.

COMMENTS This is the only rye whiskey that lets you have it at the full 101 proof and the drinker is rewarded with a whiskey of outstanding quality and complexity. Like Jim Beam straight Rye it is a classic of the genre. This, though, is not quite so rye-dominant and allows other complexities to tantalise the palate. No bar in the world should be without one or the other.

CALIFORNIA RYE

ANCHOR

Tucked away in the Potrero area of San Francisco is a distillery much better known as a brewery. This is the Anchor Steam Brewery, the founding father and inspiration to America's micro brewing industry. Its owner, Fritz Maytag, fears that he might also spawn a thousand micro distilleries, something which does not greatly appeal to him. At the moment he is America's smallest distiller and wants to stay that way.

Maytag's distillery is housed under the same roof as his spotless brewery, towards the back of the building. He is not remotely interested in making bourbon. What he is interested in is making a whiskey which perhaps America's very first whiskey distillers would easily have recognized. For that reason he uses a small copper pot still and rye as his sole grain.

That means malting it for fermentation purposes and his reward has been probably the most extraordinary new whiskey to hit the market in the last two years. It has the same effect on first-time drinkers as peaty Islay whisky might: they either love it or loathe it. Certainly, these days it is highly unusual for the taste-buds to be given such a comprehensive working over. However, Fritz has found that as the 21st-century approaches it is becoming near impossible to marry ancient practices with 20th-century law. When the first rye distillers of Maryland and Pennsylvania hung their modest copper pots over a fire, they called the resulting spirit whiskey. The last thing on their minds were such trifles as how old it was, and what it had to be called. Indeed, the whole point of the whiskey "wars" of the late 18th century was to show their anger at Federal interference.

Fritz, too, has had a problem. His first ever Federal Government-approved whiskey was a rye called Old Potrero. Less than two years old it was halfway between clear and red spirit and offered a mouthwatering fruitiness that no other bottled whiskey in the world can match. But he has had to change the labelling. He had called it rye whiskey, which according to regulations he cannot strictly do. Apparently it should be called Rye Malt, which he had no intention of calling it. And a strange Californian law means that he could not call it whiskey until it is three years old (for the rest of the country it is two). Also there is an insistence by law that rye must be matured in charred new oak barrels. Again this is something that goes against the grain because over 200 years ago barrels were used merely as containers, not conditioners, and would have been used time and time again. What he did not want Anchor Whiskey to have was that powerful oak-vanilla richness that gives bourbon its distinctiveness.

In the forthcoming years there will be more whiskey coming from the Anchor distillery, though to remain on the right side of the authorities he will not be calling it that. He might instead dub it Monongahela, the style of rye known throughout Pennsylvania two centuries ago. The words "whiskey" "rye" or "rye malt" do not have to be used, nor even virgin charred oak barrels. Thankfully for all whiskey lovers, this fascinating and delicious link with the past looks set to continue its renaissance.

Below
Old Potrero,
a revival of the
Monongahela
style by Anchor,
America's
smallest
distillery.

OLD POTRERO

NOSE Truly different from any other commercial whiskey in the world. There is ample indication of youth, maybe even a particle or two of feintiness hang in the air. But the overwhelming sense is one of beauty with evidence of a touch of pure honey, softened by honeysuckle, something you would never expect from a whiskey so young, The rye is powerful yet never overwhelming with a charming sweetness beyond the honey. A soft buzz of spice wraps it up perfectly. Astonishing stuff.

TASTE The very first note is one of sweetness and this is followed, almost immediately, by something quite extraordinary. Few whiskies manage such a tidal wave of intense flavour crashing against, over and finally through the taste-buds. It is almost overwhelming. The malted rye produces rich fruity notes and a sublime oiliness which clings to the mouth's every crevice to guarantee maximum effect. That youth and hint of feintiness can still be picked out, but it is minor league stuff against the honey-coated treat the palate is undergoing.

FINISH Very long, remains oily and there are subtle hints of chocolate adding a countering bitter-sweetness to the fruit and fading honey. It is the hardness of the rye that finally emerges and stays the course longest. Nothing less than magnificent.

COMMENTS This is the most exciting taste in world whisky at the moment. Although in limited supply, it offers whiskey connoisseurs the chance to experience something very different and truly great. There is only one way to drink this: neat, without water or ice. There really is nothing else like this around, so if you are lucky enough to spot it in a restaurant don't miss out. The youngest classic of them all.

CORN WHISKEY

There has been corn whiskey in Kentucky since the very first days settlers and prospectors set foot in those wilderness lands. Bourbon had not been invented. There was just whiskey.

Two hundred years on there is still a demand for this most simple of whiskeys. It is still made by moonshiners in Georgia, where it never really went out of fashion, Tennessee and Kentucky. That type of whiskey rarely gets the chance to progress beyond its clear spirited state, the evidence drunk before the taxman cometh and, so I have been often told, tastes all the better for it.

But despite the rise of bourbon and rye, matured corn whiskey has always been available in America, though rarely beyond. Today only the one distiller makes it, Heaven Hill.

Until the mid 80's there was a rival corn whiskey, made from out of state. That was the rich-textured, simplistic Platte Valley, once made at McCormick's distillery, Weston, Missouri. The brand still exists, only now it is the eponymous

Heaven Hill whiskey which fills the bottle. The old Weston distillery still stands today, but has been silent for a decade.

However, Heaven Hill can take pride in the corn whiskeys they offer. The most startling is JW Corn, the fruitiest I have ever encountered and showing good age and style. Much lighter, and more indicative of corn whiskey of old is Mellow Corn, a deliciously delicate brand. It just goes to prove, though, that a whiskey style so often vilified for allegedly being mutton dressed as lamb can be the belle of the ball. If you are a true student of whiskey, your education is a long way from being complete until you have mastered this particularly charming form.

DIXIE DEW • 100 PROOF:
Uncomplex, like corn bread, attractive and easy going. Delightful.

MELLOW CORN • 100 PROOF
NOSE: Soft – mellow, even, as the name promises – corn, more corn and nothing but corn. Rather attractive.

MELLOW CORN • 100 PROOF

TASTE: Astonishingly oily and rich middle. Chewable corn, attractively sweet at first with accompanying soft peppers.

FINISH: Some cinnamon-type spices arrive to give balance but do not detract from the slightly mollased sweetness. Just a little oaky vanilla turns up at the finish to give hint of bourbon.

COMMENTS: This is beautiful whiskey: if you see it, buy it. There is a softness unusual for any whiskey in the world and few are so naturally sweet. Great weight and hint of complexity, as well. Every home should keep a bottle. Altogether a delicate and highly impressive whiskey.

JW CORN • 100 PROOF

NOSE An odd nose, the corn being blanked out by strange and hefty fruit notes, mainly prunes.

TASTE Fat, sweet and lots of oaky corn and delicious peppers.

FINISH Long, amazingly oily then slightly more bitter than others. Even so, beautifully balanced.

COMMENTS: Classic corn whiskey. It just shows what happens when oak blends perfectly with something as simple as corn.

BLENDED WHISKEY

There's one final style of whiskey in America deserving of mention: blended whiskey. Whereas blended Scotch continues to account for about 94 per cent of all its nation's sales, blended bourbon accounts for only a fraction of whiskey sold by the bourbon industry. Nor does it enjoy the same high regard.

In Scotch, the lighter-character grain spirit which has been distilled to a high alcoholic strength in continuous stills, rather than a lower strength in batch all-copper pot stills, is matured for a minimum of three years. Only then is it blended in with an array of malt whiskies. In Ireland a single grain is often blended with the fruits of just a single malt or Irish pot still (that is a mixture of malted and unmalted barley peculiar to the Irish), but again only after it has matured for three years and taken on a softening character.

Blended American whiskey, however, is a lot more impatient. The "grain neutral spirits" (GNS) may have seen the inside of a barrel, but there is no specification for just how long.

However all bourbon must be aged a minimum of two years, and age must be stated on the label if it is less than four years old. In the leading blend, Kessler (by Jim Beam), the bourbon used *must* be a minimum of four years, as there is no age statement. It also reveals that grain neutral spirits account for 72.5 per cent of the blend.

In fact blended American whiskey can contain up to 80 per cent GNS or light whiskey, that's a whiskey matured in used oak barrels or new ones that have been uncharred. There are other sub-species of blended whiskey. For instance, I have from the 1930s a wonderful bottle of blended rye whiskey. That means that at least 51 per cent of the whiskey contains pure rye whiskey, the other may be GNS. Likewise any whiskey containing a mixture of at least 51 per cent bourbon and the remainder lighter whiskey or GNS would be known as "blended bourbon whiskey" or "bourbon whiskey – a blend".

I cannot say that blended American is my favourite type of whiskey. Kessler claims to be "Smooth as Silk", which I concede it is. But there is absolutely no complexity to either the nose or over-sweet taste and the finish is thin.

Not all blends use GNS as their base. Some use light whiskey, that is whiskey matured in used barrels which had they been matured in new oak would have been fit to be called bourbon. The Early Times Old Style Kentucky Whiskey is such a blend, but it rather falls down when it comes to flavour profile and finish and cuts up a little rough on the palate. My favourite of them all is Seagram's Seven Crown which is not only gentle and beautifully textured and deliciously clean on the palate but possesses some quite glorious, fluting, rye notes in the nose and taste.

265

WHERE TO VISIT

THE DISTILLERIES

Opposite
A 1950s gift
idea to promote
I W Harper –
the "Traveller"
hip-flask. Perfect
for those lonely
stretches between
distilleries.

By now it will already have become apparent that Kentucky and Tennessee are two magnificent places for the whiskey lover to visit. Not only are the distilleries fascinating to tour, but the country in which they are set is quite stunning. All that added to the genuinely warm welcome you receive guarantees a journey to remember. Maker's Mark and Labrot & Graham are musts for the visitor, two distilleries where great lengths have been taken to attract visitors to these famous homes of whiskey without tourism in any way affecting the look of the distillery inside or out.

Jack Daniels, George Dickel, Jim Beam and Wild Turkey also offer a pleasant experience for aficionados, and lovers of Four Roses may get a look around providing they make arrangements in advance. Until the recent fire Heaven Hill also offered guided tours and hope to do so again. The main no go areas are Beam's Boston

distillery, Barton, Bernheim and Early Times, though you never know what an opportunist phone call might bring.

To make life easier for the visitors to whiskey country, Kentucky distillers have in 1998 combined to create a Bourbon Trail. Maps will be provided to let the visitor know just which distillery to visit next and what special events may be held there from time to time. And just for good measure the maps will show other places or historic interest and natural beauty on the way.

THE OSCAR GETZ WHISKEY MUSEUM

No trip to Kentucky would be complete for the whiskey lover without a visit to the Oscar Getz Whiskey Museum. Set in Spalding Hall, an elegant red brick building in the heart of Bardstown, the museum offers a fascinating range of artifacts to view and gives an extraordinary insight into Kentucky's bourbon heritage. The displays include three magnificent ancient pot stills, complete with worms; and an old moonshiner's still. There are many rare old photographs of now lost distilleries and archives which the serious whiskey student can study upon request. Bourbon bottles made in around 1825 can be inspected as well as some of the first bourbon labels, dating back to around 1880. Intriguingly, some of the very old whiskey bottles still contain the whiskey made by long lost – but not forgotten – distillers.

Remarkably this golden nugget of the whiskey world is free to visit. During winter months (November 1st–April 30th) it is open Tuesday to Saturday 10am–4pm and Sunday 1pm–4pm. At all other times it is open seven days a week, Monday to Saturday 9am–5pm and Sundays 1pm–5pm

THE BOURBON FESTIVAL

Bardstown is also the venue for a whole week's celebration of America's indigenous spirit. Every year during the third week of September Kentucky distillers unite to put on a series of activities and shows which help improve people's understanding of bourbon and Kentucky life. The events range from informal tastings to country and western concerts. There are a number of fun events including the most famous of them all, where warehousemen from rival distilleries challenge each other to a barrel rolling contest.

INDEX

Page references in bold type indicate tasting notes for individual whiskeys. The following abbreviations are used in this index to indicate the distilleries from which individual brands originate:

A - Anchor AA - Ancient Age Ba - Barton Be - Bernheim ET - Early Times FR - Four Roses GD - George Dickel HH - Heaven Hill JB - Jim Beam JD - Jack Daniel LG - Labrot & Graham MM - Maker's Mark S - Seagram SW - Stitzel Weller W - Willett WT - Wild Turkey